REACH OUT TO SINGLES

REACH OUT TO SINGLES

A CHALLENGE TO MINISTRY

by
RAYMOND KAY BROWN

W'

THE WESTMINSTER PRESS
Philadelphia

Scripture quotations from the Revised Standard
Version of the Bible are copyrighted 1946, 1952,
© 1971, 1973 by the Division of Christian
Education of the National Council of the
Churches of Christ in the U.S.A., and are used by
permission.

Book Design by Dorothy Alden Smith

FIRST EDITION

Published by The Westminster Press®
Philadelphia, Pennsylvania

PRINTED IN THE UNITED STATES OF AMERICA
9 8 7 6 5 4 3 2 1

Grateful acknowledgment is made to the following:

E. P. Dutton & Co., Inc., for excerpts from *Passages,* by Gail Sheehy.
Copyright © 1974, 1976 by Gail Sheehy.
M. Evans and Company, Inc., for excerpts from *Creative Divorce,* by
Mel Krantzler. Copyright © 1973–1974 by Mel Krantzler.
The Seabury Press, Inc., for excerpts from *A Pew for One, Please,* by
William Lyon. Copyright, 1977, by William Lyon.
J. P. Tarcher, Inc., for excerpts from *The Challenge of Being Single,*
by Marie Edwards and Eleanor Hoover, © 1974, published by New
American Library.
Word Books, Publisher, for excerpts from *It's O.K. to Be Single,* edited
by Gary R. Collins.

Library of Congress Cataloging in Publication Data

Brown, Raymond Kay, 1936–
    Reach out to singles.

    Bibliography: p.
    1. Church work with single people.   I. Title.
BV639.S5B76   261.8'34   79-15495
ISBN 0-664-24270-7

Copy 2

CONTENTS

PREFACE

SINGLE ADULTS, eighteen years old and over, comprise nearly one third of the adult population in the United States. In 1976, there were 49 million single adults, of which 26 million had never been married, and 23 million were "single again." To dissect the latter number more specifically, 7.2 million are divorced, 11.8 million are widowed, and 3.8 million are separated.[1] Nearly sixty percent are women. Forty-six percent are under thirty years of age. Recent U.S. Bureau of the Census statistics indicate that more young people are remaining single longer. Single adults clearly are a factor to be reckoned with as an influential part of the adult population.

Such figures were not a part of my consciousness until a few years ago. As a pastor of a United Presbyterian Church congregation in Tacoma, Washington, I was more aware of the nuclear family and its needs. Our congregation, like so many others, aimed its primary ministry toward families and couples. We had family retreats, family nights, a couples club, and sermons on the family and marriage. Our language, in church newsletters and worship, expressed the same focus. We were little aware of the subtle ways that single adults in our midst were made to feel excluded. We weren't sure why so many singles never came to church.

One day a young woman in the congregation came in for

counseling. She indicated that she felt excluded from much of the congregation's life. "Whether you realize it or not, very few of my friends bother to come to church. They feel that the church is really only concerned about married people."

She shared some of her experiences as a single woman living in a nearby apartment village complex. When she moved to Tacoma, she wanted to establish a relationship with a local church. She had gone to several. Each time she left because there seemed to be much for married people, and little for singles. Finally, she decided to talk with a pastor about her plight. Her story would affect the direction of my ministry.

A few weeks later, at a gathering of pastors from several local congregations, I shared my concern for developing a ministry to singles in our area. Their response to the idea was rather cool. Some seemed to lack a general understanding of singles and others had "tried to start a singles group and got little or no response."

My hypothesis began to develop: there is a great gap between single adults and the institutional church. It was my growing hunch that what was true of our community was also true of many others. Many singles sense a stigma attached to them by the church about "being single." They see an institution more sensitized toward families and married persons. Traditional approaches of ministry to single adults do not seem relevant to the varying life-styles of single adults in today's society.

I decided that a good deal of consciousness-raising was necessary for me, as well as for the average congregation, regarding the needs of single adults. Until that process begins, most attempts at "a singles ministry" will remain futile and unsatisfactory, for both church leaders and a large number of single adults.

I began serious research into the needs of single adults and how the church might more adequately minister to those needs. I wanted to have more data on how local church leaders perceived the needs of single adults and how they saw the church ministering to those needs. How do single adults see their own needs? What are their perceptions concerning the church's sensitivity to those needs? I attempted to sample viewpoints and experiences from as wide a variety of singles as possible, particularly in terms of age, circumstances of singleness, and experience with the church. More than forty pastors and three hundred single adults were surveyed. Church leader responses represented a variety of theological perspectives, program styles, and congregational sizes.

Research continued through an extensive journey into literature dealing with single adults. I found very little in church publications. Only recently has there begun to exist a broader selection of literature on single adults from church circles.

Focus upon single adults through interviews and questionnaires centered primarily upon the metropolitan areas of Seattle and Tacoma, Washington. Seattle has the largest concentration of single adults, per capita, of any major metropolitan area in the United States. This provided a good arena for sampling the needs of a wide variety of singles. I am convinced that most of what we learned here is true about singles anywhere.

This book is written in the hope that it will not only provide valuable data for a more inclusive understanding of the single adult in American society today but also challenge church leaders to develop more productive ministries with adults who are single.

The first chapter, after a general assessment of the need for singles ministries, looks at basic questions behind good planning in any form of ministry. The subsequent three chapters attempt to present an overview of the pressures under which single adults live and the problems they face. These chapters are intended to help raise the consciousness of people who seek to have a better understanding of singles.

A Biblical view of singleness is explored in the fifth chapter, followed by a look at some options that might be considered in developing a ministry with single adults.

I would be remiss if I did not express my appreciation to those many single adults who, in their own emerging sense of wholeness, helped to nurture me to a broader understanding of the meaning of singleness. Their sensitivity and perspective was an inspiration. Special acknowledgments also go to the members of the Singles Seminar at the Ghost Ranch Conference Center in Abiquiu, New Mexico; to Rev. J. Graley Taylor, who urged me on in my research; to the members of the Task Force on the Single Adult in the Church of the Church Council of Greater Seattle, who helped sort through research data; to Dr. Thomas Kirkpatrick, who not only sharpened some research skills but proved to be a deep friend during some of the more trying moments of my life; and to Rev. Neal Kuyper, my patient adviser during the writing of this project. Alice Holberg typed and retyped the manuscript from my sometimes illegible longhand, producing a legible result for the publisher.

My children and my wife, Suzanne, also provided high levels of patience and support during the times when my disposition did not always merit the evidences of their love, and for that I am grateful.

R.K.B.

Spokane, Washington

1

LET'S FORM A SINGLES GROUP!

(ASKING THE RIGHT QUESTIONS FIRST)

A PASTOR looks out upon his congregation on a Sunday morning. He notices the Smith family, seated in the front pew. Behind them are the Bradleys and the Bumps. His eyes move to several other families. Then he notices Claire, a divorcée, trying to keep her two children settled. At the end of her pew Mrs. Jelinek, a widow, is seated with another widow friend. Bob Sand, a church officer who is single, ushers in two college-age women who have recently moved into the neighborhood. The pastor glances at Jim, a middle-age salesperson, seated in the back pew by himself. Jim's wife left him two weeks ago.

The pastor ponders briefly his sudden awareness of the variety of single adults present that morning. What do we offer these people? he thinks to himself. What can be done to help them face life as singles? I wish I understood their needs better. Maybe we should form a singles group. I wonder what they want.

What course should this congregation take in relating to those singles in its midst? Where does it begin? What about single adults in congregations where the leaders do not even notice them? And those in the community who have given up on the church "because of its strong family orientation"?

The church faces a challenge in approaching such questions and developing forms of ministry appropriate to the particular needs of singles. Many local congregations have been able to address these needs with sensitivity and creativity. Yet, there is still a great deal to be done, both in consciousness-raising and action. Many people, especially those who are single, feel that the surface has yet to be penetrated. Much of what is attempted by the churches is thought to be traditional and ineffective; actually an evasion of personal ministry to singles. As one observer notes:

> The established church seems to be traditional in its ways, impersonal in its approach to outsiders and even towards its own members. It appears to be like a machine that is interested more in keeping moving and keeping its gears oiled than in developing spiritual insight and experience in the lives of its members. They thus become disgruntled with the church and its practices. At this point they seek out more personal organizations, leaders who relate to them more individually and personally, who treat them as valid persons, and who communicate personalness to them. . . . Too often in the impersonal church the individual feels unwanted, rejected, and alienated.[1]

William Lyon tells of a personal friend, a former church member, who had specified several things that

> she had sought in vain to find in her local church: inspiration, recognition, warmth or affection, the opportunity to make a contribution, self-improvement, new friends—including maybe a boyfriend, and most important of all, a substitute family. She no longer believes that she can find what she needs in a church environment.[2]

Such criticisms may seem harsh. Yet they need to be heard. Like any institution, the church can easily become so concerned about its own inner workings, about its survival, that it becomes impersonal and unable to hear the cries of those who seek to be heard.

Much of the data that came back from single adults in local

churches indicated a basic lack of understanding of the needs of single adults on the part of pastors and other church leaders. Even in larger churches, where bigger staffs existed, single adults indicated that they were not really heard. A program could be popular, drawing large numbers, yet remain impersonal.

Sometimes such a lack of personalness may simply come because of size. There can easily be a dedication to run an efficient program for large numbers and slight the individuals within it.

William Lyon levels strong criticism at such tendencies in the church's ministry. He contends that pastors and parishioners who remain insensitive to the spiritual and psychological needs of single adults often do so simply out of ignorance rather than intention. Caught up in the rat race of producing programs for so many areas of need, they are not informed about the needs of single adults. Trying to maintain a program that is heavily marriage- and family-oriented, they simply neglect the single adults.

Congregations that produce well-organized, efficient programs often fail to encourage interpersonal relationships that include singles, much less other persons outside the usual church fellowship.

Many single adults are quick to agree with such criticism. However, the burden of responsibility does not fall solely upon the church. We live in a society that acts like a machine. Bureaucracy tends to permeate any institution, depersonalizing those affected by its forms.

Single adults often fail to notice the good opportunities that are offered in churches. Many singles do not know what they want, and, like many other people in our society, want to be spoon-fed with instant programs. Others are quick to judge and slow to add constructive alternatives to what they are criticizing.

Yet, the burden rests heavily upon the church to develop adequate programs that do deal with single adults. Such programs need to be sensitive and personal. There is great potential still to be tapped.

Britton Wood contends that "the church can provide one of the few opportunities for single adults to meet in a non-threatening environment."[3]

The church does face a great challenge. While valid criticism can be leveled at much of what the church has done and is doing, many good things are happening and can happen in a ministry with single adults. The church has the resources, the people, and the concern to develop many appropriate forms of ministry.

The Task Force on the Single Adult in the Church in the Seattle-Tacoma area noted in its report:

> In reaching out to singles the church will be committing itself to its own renewal. Indeed, that our task force was called into being is an indication that the contemporary church finds itself at an historical crossroads. One fork of this road points to a kind of religious community in which the family is central, and the married state the norm from which all other patterns of living and relating are deviants. *The other fork points to a kind of religious community in which the quality of one's life, rather than the outward form of one's living arrangement, is the focal point of authentic religious concern.*[4]

Today, many people seem to be seeking quality and meaning in life. They want a sense of inner direction and forms of community that are inclusive. For the single adult, this means a community that does not put a premium upon being married so much as being whole. To choose the direction that helps persons, whether single or married, to deal with the quality of life is a prime opportunity for the church.

Clearly, if the church is to be a vital force in society, it needs to include those persons whose patterns of life and thought are shaping what society is to be. The declining numbers of church members and the expanding numbers of singles suggest to us a failure on the part of the church to reach out to an increasingly important segment of people.[5]

The church does have the potential for renewal, for redirecting its style of ministry with single adults. As God's Spirit continues to work through human events, new directions of ministry will emerge. Such new forms can include singles.

Mark Lee attempts to suggest some ways in which the church can begin to express a genuine concern for single adults if it is going to minister more effectively to singles. He suggests that the church needs to:

1. Recognize that the single status is the appropriate available option to being married.
2. Relate to the interests of singles.
3. Provide full opportunity for singles to act responsibly in the life of the church.
4. Call upon Christians to keep fidelity with biblical principles relative to personal conduct.
5. Adjust the present focus of the church's ministry on the nuclear family.
6. Activate programs which will meet the needs of singles.
7. Build the church on Jesus Christ.[6]

These directions imply some changes in many established ways of thought and practice in a vast majority of local congregations. Marriage can still be valued as an important institution, yet not as the goal for every adult. Some churches will need to take serious inventory of the subtle ways in which singles are excluded from church activities because of an overemphasis upon marriage and family. It implies that singles who are already within local churches will need to become more vocal to see that their presence and influence is felt.

Speaking from an optimistic viewpoint, hopeful of the church's potential for making such changes, Britton Wood writes, "The church is the only institution that is styled to care for and welcome all persons regardless of where they are at any point in their lives."[7] Wood's statement expresses a fervent hope and belief in the church as a redemptive, inclusive community.

Anne Hagen and many others warn against the church "singling out" singles for another special group. "They should not be restricted to their own kind."[8] She adds:

> The church should avoid segregating singles as a special minority. Most singles don't want to be singled out from other adults, yet they want their particular needs considered, indeed, deserve to have these met.[9]

In some instances, special activities or groupings for single adults may be needed and wanted. At other times and locations this is just what is not wanted. The church needs to be sensitive to what the situation merits. Counselor-author Howard Clinebell has said:

> Meeting the needs of nonfamily persons is a challenge to any church. In a sense, this is the acid test of a church's person-centeredness. Can its group program be so varied, inclusive, and need-satisfying that it can provide a substitute family for the family-less?[10]

A local church concerned about developing a ministry to and with single adults within its membership and community will need to ask some basic questions before any decisions are made regarding the form of ministry to single adults.

SOME BASIC QUESTIONS
FOR DEVELOPING A SINGLES MINISTRY

What Are Our Motives and Goals?

A constant danger in the church is that it enter into particular forms of ministry without assessing its motives and goals. This often only leads to misdirected efforts and much frustration.

When I began to explore the ministry with single adults, there were persons within the congregation who questioned whether it was "worth the effort to go after singles." Single adults are often stereotyped as fickle and evasive. The large concentration of singles who lived in the apartment house complex near the church was viewed as a group that was "hard to reach."

In pursuing the concern, I began to realize what was really being said. It was that singles are "poor prospects" for church membership. Like so many local congregations, we were falling into the subtle "numbers game" which overlooks the unique needs of persons. If our concern really is for persons, then we must listen carefully for the particular biases and stereotypes that obscure that concern. If single adults are simply seen as objects for ministry, in order to "gain more members," many singles will quickly detect the motives and continue to avoid the church.

Each congregation needs to think through its reasons for exploring a stronger ministry to adults who are single. It should explore what it hopes to accomplish through such a ministry. What are its goals, its motives?

There is a great need for more adequate church involvement with single persons, and the results of such ministry can be mutually satisfying. But, as William Lyon warns, "if a church involves itself in singles' work from a base of ignorance, pater-

nalism, or a laissez-faire philosophy, neither side will benefit."[11] Lyon suggests that there are benefits both for single
adults and for the church. "The church needs single people.
It needs their energy, money, time, love, and their unique
potential for commitment."[12] While his perspective borders
on manipulation, he addresses some of the crucial concerns
regarding singles ministry.

> What is needed is for church leaders and members to develop
> an awareness and appreciation of single persons as, basically, just
> people. The single may have some special needs, but who hasn't?
> These needs can be attended to, and satisfied, without making
> a special case out of the single person who sees himself or herself
> as a person who is single, not as a single.
>   In short, what I am advocating is that the church would be
> more successful in its singles' work if it concentrated more on
> needs and less on trying to figure out what it can do to help those
> people.[13]

A church should not proceed into a singles ministry until it
can specify what goals it hopes to achieve through such a
ministry. Pastoral and staff leaders, church officers, and other
key personnel should take all the time necessary to define
motives and goals. Then, if after this kind of self-questioning,
they can delineate their purposes and goals, there is reason to
move forward.

Who Are the Singles? What Are Their Needs?

During my study it became evident that many local church
leaders lack an awareness of who the singles are in the congregation or surrounding community, much less what their needs
are.

Getting the data is an important early process. A first step
for a congregation, or group of congregations, would be to go

over the membership rolls to ascertain just how many single persons there are, and who they are. Are there more men than women? What is the age range? How many are widows or widowers? etc. The local census bureau or city planners may be able to provide data regarding community single adult concentrations.

Lyon suggests that single adults can be divided into two basic groups: those who intend to remain single (permanent singles) and those who hope not to remain single (temporary singles).

Although these two groups differ from one another in many ways, they are much more alike than they are unlike. What they have in common is what brings them together, and perhaps to the church. Some people have never really been single; they went from parents to spouse to the grave. Others have, emotionally at least, been single, alone all their lives.[14]

Determining the breakdown of singles in a particular congregation or community is important. Then some decisions might be made as to which singles to concentrate upon:

1. Young, teen-age singles who live at home?
2. College-age and post-college-age singles who live away from home?
3. The pre-spinster-age single persons in their thirties?
4. Divorcées?
5. Widows and widowers?
6. Senior citizens?
7. Religiously committed singles who may well not marry?
8. Homosexuals? Lesbians?
9. Those who go to church?
10. Any single person who happens to show up?

Defining some of the needs of single persons may be easier once a perspective is gained as to who comprises the largest concentration of those singles.

Rev. Jim Smoke, minister to single adults at the Garden Grove Community Church in California, suggests that singles have four basic needs:

1. Relational: building relationships with other singles.
2. Social Interaction: with a variety of social activities.
3. Spiritual: obtaining a sense of spiritual direction in an atmosphere that is warm, positive, nonjudgmental.
4. Educational: seminars, lectures, activities which deal directly with the needs of singles in all areas.[15]

The data presented in Chapter 3 suggest a broader scope of singles needs than Smoke's list. Some of these needs would apply to a particular category of single adult (i.e., never-married, divorced, widowed, single parent). An awareness of some of the needs that are common to most single adults is crucial in developing any singles ministry.

Many single adults, like those who are not single, do not have a grasp of their own needs. A local church may need to do its own research, data-gathering, interviewing with cooperative singles. There is very little material available presently through denominational bodies which seems to deal adequately with the needs of single adults.

Recently the General Assembly of The United Presbyterian Church U.S.A. received a recommendation from its Committee on Nurture and Fellowship concerning Single Adults and the Church. After noting that "there is an increasing number of single adults of all ages who have special needs that should be addressed by the church," the General Assembly made the recommendation that

> the Program Agency study the needs of single adults (post high school and up) of all ages in the United Presbyterian Church and in society and bring back recommendations . . . for a denominationally coordinated effort to meet those discovered needs.[16]

Until such information is made available on a larger scale by denominational agencies, local churches will have to rely on local resources and people to provide information on the needs of singles. Ultimately, this may be the best resource into a more personalized ministry, anyway. Outside resources can provide the broader scope of experience, research, and perspective. But the local church should make those decisions which best fit its situation.

It needs to be stressed that single adults should, if possible, be a part of the data-gathering process. They may be persons from the local church or outside it. They can often be most articulate regarding their needs and concerns.

Once motives, goals, and singles and their needs have been identified, it is possible to move toward a determination of the form, or forms, which a possible ministry might take in a given locality.

Really to understand the needs of single adults seems simple, but it is extremely difficult. Let us proceed, in the next section, to look at the world of the single adult, focusing on some of the pressures and needs commonly experienced.

2

SURELY YOU PLAN TO GET MARRIED!

(GROWING UP SINGLE IN A PAIRING CULTURE)

A PERVASIVE PRESSURE experienced by adults who are single is the expectation that "they all eventually want to get married." At an early age little girls learn that the kiss of a prince will make them live happily ever after. Little boys are told that a kiss from the right girl can transform them from a frog to a prince.

Young girls read that a knight on a white horse will save them from a dragon. Boys learn that saving the right young lady will win the hand of the king's beautiful daughter.

The pressure to pair is often subtle but constant.

The novel *Sheila Levine Is Dead and Living in New York* is about a young Jewish girl who felt such pressure. Sheila responds by trying hard to find a mate. Her pursuit is thwarted in nearly every direction she turns. Musing about how early the pressure comes, she notes how people commented at her birth:

> August 12, thirty years ago . . . "My, what a beautiful baby."
> . . . "So, it's a girl, Manny? You know what that means, you have to pay for the wedding. . . ." One day old! One day old, and they're talking about weddings.
> Mom, you told a story! "I took Sheila to the doctor when she was a month old, and I was so upset because she had a tiny little scratch on her face. . . . You know what the doctor told me? He

said, 'Don't worry. Don't worry yourself, Bernice. It'll be gone
by the time she gets married.'" Married? There it is again, Pop,
and I was one month old![1]

Through her experiences she concludes that "everything
comes in pairs but Sheila Levine."[2] Still she kept on trying,
hopping into bed with every man who showed any interest in
her. But nothing seemed to work.

> I did everything I could to get married. I went to peace marches
> in the cold. . . . Maybe I'd meet a nice peacenik who wanted
> marriage. I went to rallies and night courses. . . . I went to every
> party I was invited to, every party I ever heard of. I went on a
> ski weekend and sprained my nose in the snow. I tried.
>   . . . The only thing I didn't do was move to Australia, where
> the men outnumber the women. . . .
>   Do you have any idea how much money I have spent trying
> to get married? I estimate at least fifteen thousand dollars.[3]

Sheila Levine later attempted suicide. The pressure to pair
became too great for her. She fit a stereotype well—that she
should get married. And she tried hard, unsuccessfully.

Newsweek magazine, June 16, 1973, carried an article entitled "Games Singles Play." In the article, singles, primarily
younger in age, were described as an intense, swinging segment
of society. Commenting on the article, Marie Edwards and
Eleanor Hoover note, according to the perspective of the article:

> Behind all the "intensely ritualized" enjoyment, behind the
> drinking, dancing, sailing, and martinis, bikinis, poolside stereos,
> and saunas, there may be detected, if one just looks, the same
> old loneliness, despair, second-class personhood, and longing to
> be married. The implication is that it is probably okay to be
> fun-loving and single until you are thirty, but then, "Forget it!
> . . . we know that you, behind that suntan, are single, lonely and
> you want to be married."[4]

Everywhere the single adult looks, it seems to be a couples world. Singles are urged by authors, advertisements, parents, and therapists to raise their sex quotient, get involved, shape up, be more open, more honest, more intimate. And above all, find Mr. Right or Miss Wonderful and get married! Even books supposedly extolling the single life are in reality thinly disguised manuals on making do until "the right person" comes along. Seldom do singles find the suggestion that a single is anything but an incomplete couple or that to be single can be a fulfilling, rewarding, freely chosen life-style, rather than a fearful, lonely waiting ground for marriage.

Author Terri Williams suggests that there may be two myths associated with the pairing-marriage pressure in our society. The Myth of Fulfillment is communicated most extensively by the mass media. It suggests that "you will never be really happy or fulfilled until you have found the right person to love." This Myth of Normality is communicated most extensively by the people one meets every day. Through their words, tone of voice, and expressions, they suggest that "normal, well-adjusted people get married." The obsession to attract, to date, to woo and win strikes even the grade school child. By the teen years, the obsession is well established. "And of course, people with an obsession are an easy target for salesmen."[5] The author suggests that society's obsession with erotic love pushes into marriage many people who are not ready, not able to assume the responsibilities or privileges of marriage.

Many single adults today have begun to resist such pairing pressure. They are not opting for marriage as the only answer to human fulfillment and wholeness. Some are skeptical of the institution of marriage. Many who had an unpleasant experience in a first or second marriage are simply not willing to "make another mistake." And some have simply resolved that they may never get married.

These people still experience the typical stereotypes and

insinuations about marriage from friends, relatives, business associates, clergy, and the media. But more and more are finding the single life-style suitable as a new territory in which to dwell. They see the structure of society beginning to shift. They see a growing awareness on the part of many people toward an acceptance of single adulthood.

Carole Klein, in *The Single Parent Experience*, raises the question of how we help people adapt to this shifting social structure:

> How do you socialize people into a world where the structures are shifting? These are different times from those in which our lives were measured by generationally familiar way stations. We are almost totally separating ourselves from the idea that tomorrow is only an extension of yesterday, or even of today. It used to be that parents would aim their children toward a life that was perhaps more ambitious than their own, but was in its most important ways recognizable. Country doctors wanted their sons to be big city specialists. Mothers who lived in five-room apartments hoped their daughters would marry well and move to ten-room houses.[6]

Those times have changed in many ways. Caught in the future shock are not only mothers and fathers but many of the institutions of our society. Traditionally they operated from the premise that every red-blooded boy and girl in the United States would want to grow up to be like Mommy and Daddy. The shock waves from the women's liberation movement have certainly found their effect on such traditional ideas. Edwards and Hoover have this comment on the shifting institution of marriage:

> We have lock-stepped through history so long in a Noah's Ark lineup of twosomes that it may be difficult to grasp that one of the emergent, really liberating ideas of our time may well be the final lifting of singlehood from a weary waiting ground for mar-

riage to a new status as a thoroughly viable, rewarding, enjoy-able, creative, and satisfying alternative to marriage.[7]

What we have experienced in recent years has been a whole plurality of new styles: smaller families, the rise of communal life, a new openness regarding homosexual relationships, a liberation from traditional male and female roles, and alternative styles of marriage. Demographer Paul Glick, after examining some of these changing patterns, noted:

> The shrinking household size and the growing number of small households consisting of single-parent families, unmarried couples, or persons living entirely alone are evidence that large families are no longer regarded with favor by many persons and that new life-styles are being tried by persons who want to learn whether the new ways are more satisfying to them than the more conventional patterns. Some of the living arrangements with increasing numbers of adherents are bringing unrelated persons into closer companionship, whereas more of them are providing at least temporary relief from contacts with relatives that are regarded as too close for comfort.[8]

The idolatry of the family which has characterized much of our recent history is being challenged. Institutions that were created to serve the family must reconsider their basic premises in order to relate to a changing culture. They may not abandon the family, but include alternative life-styles that encompass single adults.

Looking at some of the new patterns forcing such a change, Glick says that "the most rapid increase in household formation since 1960 has occurred among young adults with no relatives present. But the numerical increase has been much larger among elderly persons living alone." He goes on to note that "one out of four of the 143,000 unmarried couples in 1970 were women who had a male partner 'living in.' "[9] Among older couples, a substantial portion of widowed persons were living in this manner in order to avoid losing survivor benefits through remarriage. The sharp increase in the employment of women, coupled with the decline in childbirth, both signal expanding roles open to women outside the home. "The excess of marriageable women in the last few years may have contributed as much to the development of the women's movement as the ideology of the movement has contributed to the increase in singleness."[10]

If Glick and Edwards and Hoover are correct, the pairing pressure that has pushed many people toward marriage may have to give way to some new emerging styles in our culture which are more inclusive of single adults.

Singles and the Church

What about the institutional church? What role will it play in shaping the future and carrying out a ministry that includes adults who are married and those who are single either by circumstances or by choice?

For the most part, single adults generally feel that the church has geared its ministry toward those who are married and toward nuclear family units. The average congregation has placed a good deal of emphasis on family and couples retreats, couples groups, and family nights. As Donald Allen observes:

> The congregations today are clearly organized to emphasize the supremacy of the family unit. Family night suppers assume that those not living in family units will receive a welfare-like invitation from some kind, benevolent family so that the single person can come and act as though he is one of the family. The Church "thinks" family where possible in its election to persons of leadership, program planning, and building usage.[11]

So we see that many single adults who attempt to participate in local churches experience an institutional style that equates marriage with responsible adulthood. Marriage is held up as that ideal state of human existence, "instituted by God" and therefore sacred and inviolate. Thus, those who are unmarried tend to feel left out, outcast in terms of the social calendars of most congregations. With the emphasis upon marriage as the ideal state, it is little wonder that many singles have to grapple with feelings of inadequacy and incompleteness as human beings. Many of them conclude that there is no place for them in the church.

Also, with the alternative life-styles being explored by many of the singles community, particularly those of younger age, there is a natural hesitancy to participate in an institution that has traditionally condemned anything that deviates from its accepted norm.

Many singles have concluded that the church has become insensitive to their needs.

While doing research on single adults, I surveyed more than three hundred single persons. Some were participants in community-sponsored singles groups (Parents Without Partners, YMCA, etc.), while others were in church-sponsored groups. Each was given a questionnaire that contained these questions: "How would you rate the church's sensitivity to your needs as a single person?" and "How would you characterize or rate your experience with the church as a single adult?" Each participant was asked to respond on a scale from 1 (unsatisfactory) to 5 (very satisfactory).

Although the community groups claimed as much knowledge of the church as church groups did, they found it more "unsatisfactory" in terms of sensitivity to one's needs as a single person. Fifty percent of the singles in community groups checked one of the "unsatisfactory" scales. It should also be noted that nearly twenty-four percent of the community singles participants did not bother to give a rating. Does this further indicate their lack of interest or low degree of participation in the church?

It is my observation that while many singles choose to participate in a congregation, they do so feeling that the church is not aware of their particular needs. They are often expected to participate in established programs, but seldom does anyone seek to discover what is really important to them, or where they are hurting, or what excites them. Many single adults seem to have found a way to participate to a level in their church, but that level seems to be at the surface.

Is It Acceptable to Be Single?

Singles frequently experience in the life of the church assumptions about the meaning of human life. One basic assumption is that humans are created for marriage and having children. Often such thinking is subtle but strong. They hear it in sermons and prayers, and read about it in worship bulletins. They observe that couples groups, adult education courses, and family retreats are geared for the coupled. The "pairing pressure," which they encountered from early days in society, confronts them also in the church.

Our Judeo-Christian heritage has built into it a stress on marriage and family. As Emil Brunner writes:

> Marriage is the "school" of community, created by God, in which man can "learn" that he cannot live as an individual, but only insofar as he is bound with the other, as also that each one of us has received his or her own life from such a connexion between two persons.[12]

Marriage seems to be a part of "the natural order" of God's creation. Our Biblical-theological roots lay hold of this assumption, often to the exclusion of the person who is not married.

One way that the church historically has affirmed the single life-style is to hold celibacy up as an option. Celibacy is defined as "the state of being unmarried" (*Webster's New World Dictionary,* 1957). Its secondary meaning has to do with a person who has taken a religious vow to remain single.

Traditionally, we have thought of Jesus as being celibate.

Celibacy in the New Testament was allowed as a life-style for the Christian. In I Cor., ch. 7, Paul presents his argument for celibacy, suggesting that "a man does well not to marry" (v. 1).

> I would like you to be free from worry. An unmarried man concerns himself with the Lord's work, because he is trying to please the Lord. But a married man concerns himself with worldly matters, because he wants to please his wife; and so he is pulled in two directions. An unmarried woman or a virgin concerns herself with the Lord's work, because she wants to be dedicated both in body and spirit; but a married woman concerns herself with worldly matters, because she wants to please her husband. (I Cor. 7:32–34, Today's English Version)

Paul's emphasis on doing "the Lord's work," especially as an unmarried person, may have been largely due to his eschatological concern at the time of his writing. It was most important for Paul that the Christian be concerned with spiritual matters. Anything that deterred one from giving full allegiance to the Lord's work, as he saw marriage doing, should be avoided if possible.

Gradually, however, Paul's writings begin to reflect a change in his thinking, as he realized that the Parousia would not come in his time. In later writings, such as Eph. 5:21f.; Col. 3:18–19, he urges husbands and wives to love one another. He uses the relationship between husband and wife to illustrate the relationship between Christ and the church.

Roy Fairchild, noting this double message of Paul's, writes:

> On the subject of celibacy, Paul is confusing to our modern mind. It was a subject on which he blew hot and cold. Marriage,

to be sure, was a God-given status ordained to be a permanent union. It was not sinful to enter into this estate; and yet it was a second-best condition as far as he personally was concerned. He would simply rather have persons remain unattached as he was. "The unmarried are to live blameless lives of self-control; and he puts this into ultimate terms: 'Do you not know that your body is a temple of the Holy Spirit within you, which you have from God? You are not your own; you were bought with a price. So glorify God in your body.' (I Cor. 6:19–20.)"[13]

Paul's regard for celibacy as a better way of life for those who had a gift for it was strong. He evidently felt he had such a gift. His aim was reasonably clear: he wished to make sure that Christians were able to give uncompromising attention to things of the Spirit.

On the whole, however, much of the New Testament shows a suspicion of celibacy. There were instances where it seemed to be allowed, aside from Paul's admonition. Clerical celibacy emerged as one way in which the church affirmed the vocation of celibacy. Pierre L'Huillier describes some of the earliest evidences of that practice:

> The early church allowed ordination of married men and marriages of ordained men below deacons. Occasionally deacons were allowed to marry. Until the 4th century married men were consecrated bishops but the custom of restricting the episcopacy to monastics developed since the bishop was considered mystically married to his church. Sexual relations were also considered impediments to celebrating the Holy Mysteries. In the West, under papal leadership, married men were excluded from the priesthood. In the East, continence was praised but mandatory priestly celibacy was rejected in view of the earlier tradition.[14]

Further tracing some of the origins of clerical celibacy, Charles Frazee notes:

A common connection between sexual abstinence and ritual purity was espoused and enforced by appeals to the Old Testament. Not until the fourth or fifth centuries, however, did the church officially proclaim clerical celibacy. The feudal system reinforced demands for clerical celibacy since a married priesthood provided priestly heirs that could be further controlled by lay investiture. Opposition to clerical celibacy culminated in demands by Gregory the Great and decrees by the First and Second Lateran Councils.[15]

Through the centuries there have been Christian options to marriage. Celibacy is one of those options. It is still offered as a choice today. The monastic and priestly orders have lost their appeal as the vocation of singleness in serving Christ and the church. These options do not seem to be adequate to deal with the complexity of single adult needs today.

These options get quickly drowned out by the loud voices espousing marriage. As one Christian book on marriage for teens puts it: "The plan of the Creator is marriage, not singleness. . . . The plan of God is marriage. Singleness for religious service is a cultural tradition and not the plan of God."[16] This not so subtle message has its effect on the single person. It not only says to the never-married that they are "not complete," but it pushes its way into the face of the divorced person as having "failed." When the church reinforces that sense of failure many people who experience the trauma of divorce feel that they must quietly step away.

> Statistics do not reveal the personal pain, guilt, feelings of abandonment, rejection, and alienation from God and people. Few churches are able to minister to those who have been touched by this "plague." Instead there is embarrassed silence.[17]

At a time of need, church and society hold out no helping hand to divorced men or women experiencing the loss that comes with the death of a relationship. Despite the fact that almost one out of every two marriages in this country will eventually break up, the church and many other social institutions still cling to the belief that nice people don't get divorced. Divorce is accepted among the exotics of our society: film stars, television performers, and the jet-setters, but it is not for "real people," particularly if they are in the church!

This inability to come to grips with reality makes it awkward when someone in the church gets divorced. Because of the emphasis upon marriage as an institution established by God "till death do us part," divorce is hard to cope with. The trauma of this experience will be explored later.

All of this illustrates how ill-equipped the church seems to be to deal with the single adult. Much of this lack of understanding seems to be unintentional. Because of the traditional focus on marriage and family, the needs and concerns of single adults are blurred in the understanding of many well-meaning church people. The common assumptions—that we are all meant for marriage, that marriage is the highest order in God's creation, and that divorce is failure—all operate subtly to say to the single person, "You have to be married to be fully understood and accepted."

Howard Clinebell observes:

> A strong family-oriented emphasis unwittingly creates an excluding climate which tends to increase the heavy loneliness load of such persons. Meeting the needs of nonfamily persons is a challenge to any church. In a sense, this is the acid test of a church's person-centeredness. Can its group program be so varied, inclusive, and need-satisfying that it will provide a substitute family for the family-less?[18]

Clinebell's statement gets at the heart of what happens in many congregations. That strong family-oriented emphasis unwittingly creates the excluding climate. When a single person walks through the doors of a church he or she is met with an emphasis that seems oblivious of anyone outside of a family setting. To be a part of that congregation's life, the single person may try to adapt. The other option is to move away.

Many churches claim to be person-centered in their mission and ministry. They want to be inclusive and need-satisfying. As Clinebell notes, "meeting the needs of nonfamily persons is a challenge to any church."[19]

3

YOU MUST BE LONELY A LOT

(SOME COMMON SINGLES NEEDS)

A SINGLE ADULT may be defined as a person who has never married, or is in marital separation, divorced, or widowed. Singles share with other adults many of the same needs: a sense of personal identity and self-worth, a faith that is sustaining, a sense of direction, and a satisfying form of employment.

Yet, there are needs that seem unique to single persons or that affect them in a particular way.

In the course of my study, I was asked to serve, and subsequently to chair, a task force on the Single Adult in the Church. This task force was jointly sponsored by the Church Council of Greater Seattle and the Associated Ministries of Tacoma-Pierce County. Members of the task force had a wide range of interest and experience with single adult ministries. They encompassed a variety of age levels. Many were single adults. Over one half of the group was directly associated with singles work either in a community or a church-sponsored agency.

After a year and a half of research and writing, the group prepared a report on single adult needs with recommendations for utilization by individuals, churches, and community groups. Much of the material in this chapter is based on the task force report. I have taken the license to rearrange it and to supplement its insights. It is not my intent to be exhaustive, but rather, to give in broad strokes the most common singles needs, highlighting a few of these along the way.

The single adult, like any other person, has to make it in a world of relationships. One soon finds that relationships can be shallow or deep, exploitive or fulfilling, dull or full of energy and life. The factor which might be different for the single person is that a good deal of initiative must be taken to develop good, healthy relationships. While much of our society looks to marriage as the chief means of fulfilling life's purposes, the single person may be forced to seek a broader scope of relationships.

Those singles who are happy with their singleness seem to have begun to satisfy one of their main concerns, developing an affirmation of their singleness.

Developing a Sense of Singleness

In their book, *The Challenge of Being Single,* Marie Edwards and Eleanor Hoover challenge some of the negative assumptions about singleness. They propose some healthy ways in which single adults can begin to structure their personal lives in such a way as to feel good about their singleness.

The single adult must develop a sense of singleness and self-worth in a society that puts a premium upon marriage as a gauge for defining one's worth. Learning to roll past the pressures and insinuations about marriage may be a difficult task for many. Yet there are many in our culture who are noticing a new trend on the singles scene. Columbia University anthropologist Herbert Passin has observed: "For the first time in human history the single condition is being recognized as an acceptable life-style for anyone. It is finally becoming possible to be both single *and* whole."[1]

Working out a positive sense of singleness is not an easy task in a society where marriage is the norm. The church has not done much to assist the single adult to affirm singleness as a valid life-style alongside of marriage. The single person has to work this through in spite of the church's silence on the subject.

Having a support group to which one can relate can be a positive aid toward building self-respect. Such a group can provide the person with positive imaging of his or her strengths and weaknesses. It can prove to be a testing ground for constructive new life patterns. Sometimes those support groups have to be created by the single person since they are not readily available.

Reaching out to new friends is a necessary skill for the single adult.

> For the single, there is no ready-made confidant always on the scene. He has to pick as friends people who really meet his needs —needs which may change dramatically at various points in his life. Since a single can't fall back on the married relationship, he must learn to make the right friends and be the right kind of friend in order to satisfy the various emotional hungers which all human beings share.[2]

Friends often become the single's family. This is not a family built around kinship or marriage but around real preference, shared interests, and genuine affection.

Good friends allow us to be ourselves while we enjoy their company. And, in times of crisis, friends can provide support. They can be a valuable means in sharing one's life and keeping one's mind alive and ideas expanding.

> If you allow someone to understand you, all the endless role-playing, routinized remarks and behavior can be left behind. You can permit yourself to appear as you really are to someone

else, and this is one of the most effective and pleasurable ways
known of accepting and affirming yourself. By providing, accepting, clarifying, reflecting, and occasionally correcting our "real"
feelings and thoughts, particularly those we are still struggling
with, friends help us see and understand ourselves.[3]

A negative self-image seems to keep many single adults from
building constructive relationships with others or affirming
their own identity.

Consciousness-raising among single adults has been on the
increase in the past couple of years. Single adults are gaining
an awareness and pride in their corporate singleness.

One positive expression of that pride is found in "The Singles Manifesto" (see the Appendix).[4] Its articles seek to promote a positive attitude toward self, others, and society from
the viewpoint and corporate experience of single adults.

Coping with Loneliness

The late Dag Hammarskjöld, a single adult, once wrote:
"Pray that your loneliness may spur you into finding something
to live for, great enough to die for."[5] For Hammarskjöld, as
well as for countless other single adults, loneliness is continually
present in one's life. To find a satisfactory way of coping with
it is not easy.

> Once we have discovered who we are, we long to share that self
> in an intimate relationship with another. For many people this
> intimate relationship is marriage. Yet this is not automatic.
> Many marriages know no bonds of intimacy beyond physical
> coupling, while many single persons, aside from sexual union,
> have found the deepest sharing within friendship.[6]

Tragically, our society views loneliness as a negative or debili-
tating experience. To many people it connotes rejection, failure, not being desirable enough to merit the company of an-

other. In our society we see ourselves in terms of how others see us. So when no one is around to validate our existence we almost feel we don't exist. The loneliness that sets in is almost unbearable.

One unmarried woman wrote: "My hardest to handle problem, as an unmarried woman of 30–35 years, with a semiprofessional working status, high standards of personal conduct . . . has been that awful sense of aloneness, of being left out, of being unwanted."[7]

In "The Journey Isn't Over," Wes Bryan describes some of the pain he experienced following his divorce. He deals with the question of what to do with his sense of aloneness: "Most of my life I have chosen to run from it, refusing to acknowledge its existence or at least hoping to minimize it through activity."[8]

Some people experience loneliness and isolation partly because they avoid intimacy. For the single adult who has been hurt by a bad marriage, intimacy with another may be difficult. Loneliness increases. Letha Scanzoni and Nancy Hardesty describe people who become almost paralyzed by this sense of isolation:

> They just sit around in a "blue funk," a state of suspended animation, waiting for some man to somehow take them from the shelf and put them back into the center of "real life." Others try various ways to avoid loneliness through overindulgence in food, sleep, drugs, or alcohol. They develop hypochondria, they seek forgetfulness in a ceaseless round of meaningless activities, they bury themselves in overwork. Some simply refused to meet the challenge and retreat into infantile dependency on parents or relatives. Yet the problem remains, a gnawing hole in the middle of life.[9]

Lonelyhearts clubs frequently attempt to capitalize on lonely people.[10] There are presently no laws to eliminate the exploi-

tive business from advertising. Lonely people see an ad, make
a phone call, and then pay what is required in the hope that
their need for companionship will be met.

I read several hundred complaints filed through the Better
Business Bureau of Tacoma by disgruntled people. Most of
them paid a fee of at least one hundred dollars to the lonelyhearts club. They were promised a certain number of dates per
month for a given number of months.

One agency, Loneliness Anonymous, had a motto, "If you
are lonely, get to know another lonely person." The ad read,
"The buyers have to be tenderhearted, with an empathy for
lonely people." The customer was promised companionship
after paying one hundred dollars. Yet several customers reported they received no names after paying the fee.

Another agency, Dateline, a nationwide dating service, operating out of Dayton, Ohio, receives a twenty-five-dollar annual
membership fee from thousands of lonely people. It promises
"one referral for each month of membership."

Computer dating has recently grown as a means of helping
lonely people seek "the right match." The Better Business
Bureau Bulletin has warned:

> Computer dating or computer matching is now a business opera-
> tion involving long-term contracts of $259 or more. Current
> advertising is aimed at single or divorced persons and plays on
> the psychology of loneliness and the dream of the perfect date.[11]

Despite warnings like this a rising number of people continue
to seek such help to satisfy their loneliness.

Loneliness may strike the single adult at any time: during a
holiday, on weekends, especially on Sundays. It comes when
one is sitting alone in church or eating in a crowded restaurant.
It comes when one crawls into bed at night or when one is sick.

Loneliness can be devastating, or it can be turned into an
experience of growth. The Indian philosopher Krishnamurti

said, "When you are willing to face what *is*, then the loneliness comes to an end because it is completely transformed."[12] Bruce Larson writes that there seem to be two prevalent myths about loneliness:

> The first myth is that single people are the most lonely.
> I would say that I have never heard more intense experiences of loneliness than those described by many of the married people to whom I have listened over the years.
> The second myth about loneliness is that Christians with enough faith should never be lonely.[13]

He goes on to suggest that "loneliness is a precious gift." One of the values of loneliness is that it drives us into relationships—with God, and our neighbor. Mel Krantzler, making a similar observation, notes that when single persons start to flex their emotional muscles as independent people and gain confidence in their own ability to take care of themselves, two things start to happen that help dissipate loneliness and the fear of solitude:

> We clarify the needs which we can fulfill ourselves from those which only others can meet, and we begin to like ourselves more. We stop thinking of moments of solitude as accusations of our worthlessness and start to welcome them as valuable periods for reflection and personal growth.[14]

Being alone but not lonely is a challenge for the single person to meet. As Edwards and Hoover make the distinction:

> Loneliness can be defined as an acute longing for companionship, a feeling of bleakness, of isolation, and of being cut off from others in an uncomfortable, even despairing way. Being alone, on the other hand, means simply being by one's self. It can make you miserable—if you can only see it in terms of loneliness—or it can be quite enjoyable, a source of infinite possibilities once you appreciate the positive uses of being by yourself.[15]

Writing about middle-aged people who have to learn to live alone, Gail Sheehy observes:

> People who are alone in middle age may be ready to accept that learning to live alone is not just transitionally good; it can also be essentially good. Especially if one's light has been eclipsed by a dominant personality or if, having existed for many years as that corporate entity known as the couple, one has no idea if the resources are there to survive as an individual, it can be a self-affirming experience to discover that the answer is yes.[16]

Single adults seeking to come to grips with their loneliness can be helped. There are constructive avenues for both understanding their loneliness and growing through it. Keeping a chart or journal of feelings over a period of several weeks is a helpful way of examining trends and what triggers loneliness. Talking to someone who cares, doing something physical, changing one's inner pace, or helping someone else are constructive patterns. Many singles are learning the value of solitude, meditation, reading, or a hobby. Participating in social functions with other singles can be a natural outlet, though many singles warn against the futility and shallowness experienced at singles bars, discotheques, and some singles groups.

In addition to developing a sense of singleness and coping with loneliness, the single adult must come to grips with such relational needs as working through feelings of loss and grief. For the separated or divorced, that also might involve handling recurring feelings of failure and guilt. For the widowed person, it can involve working through feelings of abandonment and anger. Learning to love again, reaching out in order to build and maintain relationships, and establishing healthy degrees of intimacy are all a part of the singles need for relationships.

Finding a Sense of Community

All persons must come to their own sense of identity and to terms with themselves in their times of aloneness. Nancy Hardesty describes that pursuit:

> They search for security, a place to belong, a home, a "family" in which to live. They reach out for intimacy, for closeness, touch, union with another. They strive for achievement, a sense of accomplishment, of mission, to give life meaning.[17]

"A place to belong, a home, a 'family,' " expresses the need for community sought by most single adults. Many do not know what they want. Their frantic search for a place to belong can be seen by the myriad fads they fall into, often gaining little more than superficial acceptance.

Others find their community from a variety of different sources, some of which prove more satisfactory than others.

In research with singles several forms of community emerged which help to satisfy feelings of loneliness.

Friends obviously play a large part in the satisfaction of loneliness for the single adult (50 percent of those who responded). The church, as a form of community, scored low (10.2 percent).

By contrast, only 18.2 percent of those who were participants in church singles groups listed the church as a satisfying outlet. This would seem to indicate that the degree of satisfaction obtained by singles in the church is often low.

David Riesman's description of "the lonely crowd" might be a fitting description of the way some singles view the lack of community in many churches. It is highly possible to be present in a large group and still not have a sense of community.

GETTING CONTROL OF ONE'S LIFE

For many adults the experience of singleness comes rather abruptly. A spouse may die or be killed, and the widow is quickly thrown into a world where she has to make decisions she may previously not have had to make by herself. The same may be true of the divorced person. Handling such matters as finances, insurance, legal documents, home and auto repairs, or where to live, can be overwhelming. Likewise the single man may be thrust into the role of a meal planner, housekeeper, in addition to the above. Single parenthood has its own set of demands, especially when there are young children involved.

The demands may come so quickly that one can almost feel as though life is out of control. Getting control again may be the biggest challenge that will face the person who is suddenly single. Mel Krantzler writes:

> Living creatively in the present means accepting yourself for what you are—not what you think you should be, or wish you were, or fear you are—but the sum total of your actions, thoughts, and feelings now, at this point in time. It means accepting the responsibility for controlling one's own life. It means having the courage to ask, "What do I want out of life?" without feeling guilty.[18]

As the single seeks to gain control, there are three areas that commonly must be faced: determining a set of goals and priorities for oneself, finding a career that satisfies, and gaining enough financial security to make it within the system.

Determining Life's Goals

Being faced with a new condition of singleness often forces men and women to look at themselves in a new way. It can be a time to take stock of where one has been and where one wants to go. Goals and priorities can be set.

Jean had been married forty years when her husband died of cancer. During their marriage, her husband handled all financial matters, including investments and income taxes. She had counted on him for the major decisions in these areas.

His death left her completely disoriented regarding such matters. She felt ill-equipped for the task before her. Where was she headed? She now had some decisions to make about herself.

Many single persons, particularly women, find their new condition of singleness to be a time of growth. Some things shared as a couple in marriage may have been unsatisfactory, but never admitted. Women often find a new dimension to themselves that was hidden behind a facade of wife, or a "homemaker" stereotype.

Persons engulfed by everyday pursuits tend to avoid taking "the long view" of life. Goals are unclear and short-range.

Jim Smoke notes:

> Assuming responsibility for one's future sets one free to explore new things, ideas, situations, and to establish short-term and long-term goals. Constructive goal-setting is the ability to reach future goals by experiencing the excitement and incentive of short-term goals.[19]

Edwards and Hoover further emphasize the value of determining life's goals as a single adult:

> Having goals gives purpose to life, contributes to this pleasure, and helps us order our priorities—in people, activities, experiences, work, time. This, in turn, helps us distinguish between what is important to us and what is not.[20]

A person faced with myriad demands and expectations will find that goal-setting can be helpful. A person who knows what he or she wants is less likely to be coerced by the expectations of family, friends, or society at large. Those churches or agencies

which provide guidelines for goal-setting offer a valuable service.

Radical changes often come to persons in their later years,
and are frequently due to changes in circumstance: "Sometimes an awareness of the meaning and purpose of life strikes
people when they reach middle age and become concerned
with the finiteness of their lives. It also happens frequently in
the wake of a crisis like divorce or widowhood."[21]

The church certainly could be of more assistance to persons
at such a time. Drawing upon the skills of professional business
persons, educators, counselors, clergy, and single adults who
have become adept at goal-setting and value clarification would
prove helpful to the single adult seeking to gain control of his
or her life situation. Providing people and printed resources as
well as listening concern is an open avenue. Drawing upon the
theological insights of God's providence in our lives would help
provide spiritual strength during such a process.

Having a Career That Satisfies

Employment ranks as a major concern for many single persons. Often those who enter the employment market as a result
of divorce, widowhood, military discharge, or change in place
of residence have no idea as to what types of jobs they are
qualified to fill. They need help to understand pay scales and
career possibilities, what extra benefits to look for—such as
overtime, vacation plans, medical insurance, life insurance,
automatic or earned pay increases, job stability, and pension
plans. More crucial than informational problems are the feelings of depression, guilt, self-doubt, self-consciousness, and pes-
simism, which often hinder the single person who suddenly
finds himself or herself in the job market.

Yet, it still might be stated that many single people today
have great opportunities in the area of employment. They have

the freedom to move, to choose, to change, and to pursue work they most enjoy. This is especially true of singles who have no children. Those who have children often experience limits to their maneuverability. However, children are more flexible than we realize, and need not hinder this freedom unnecessarily.

To find work that one enjoys as well as a salary that is adequate is another matter. Edwards and Hoover have learned from singles who attend their "Challenge" workshops that discriminations still exist against singles in hiring practices. They speak of the top job market as "the executive washout."[22] "Most companies follow the general rule that married people are a better investment in terms of responsibility, dependability, and staying power."[23] A survey of fifty major corporations by the national magazine *Single* found substantial evidence of discrimination against the unmarried. Although eighty percent of the responding companies asserted that marriage was not essential to upward mobility, a majority indicated that only two percent of their executives—including junior management personnel—were single.[24] There are exceptions, of course. Single women often find that they are given preference over married women on the notion that they are more in need of work. Once hired, many single women discover that they are not taken seriously by the employers.

Many women who are not professionally trained for a job find that they must settle for jobs that are available. Often these are at a pay scale far below what they require for living expenses or desire for satisfaction. Department stores, fast-food services, and domestic jobs do not tend to provide satisfactory pay or variety for most. Women who are in their late-middle or elderly years, and who have not previously or recently been employed full time, find employment prospects particularly frightening.

Job prospects for single men likewise are less than satisfying.

Generally speaking, single men are often the last to be hired, the last to be promoted, and the first to be fired. This is particularly true in the corporate suite. The *Wall Street Journal* reports, for example, that only 2 percent of all top executives are single, while 33 percent of all adult males are single.[25]

Many singles are being advised to seek jobs with newer and smaller companies which are eager for growth and whose hiring practices are more apt to be based on talent, training, and experience than on marital status. Others are finding work in fields or professions in which they can be self-employed.

Assertiveness training, particularly for divorced women, can help in finding a satisfactory career. A person fully aware of his or her full powers has the confidence to seek out the kind of work that will be fulfilling. The world of work, like the rest of life, is changing rapidly today. It presents more options than many people who are afraid of self-direction might think.

One area where the church can assist single adults is in career-planning and employment exploration. Being sensitive to the frustrations involved, as well as providing practical assistance (references, job contacts, etc.), can demonstrate to the single adult that the church really is concerned.

Financial Security and the System

One of the biggest hurdles for the single in gaining control of his or her life has to do with finances. There are stereotypes about singles having more money to spend. *U.S. News & World Report* highlighted singles as "40 Million Free Spenders," noting that "single people—either divorced, widowed, or never-married—make up the largest concentrated pool of sales prospects in the country today."[26] The article compared the average incomes for full-time, year-round workers in 1973, citing figures issued by the U.S. Department of Labor. The average income for singles was $9,300, as compared with an average of $11,900 for a married person.

Single adults say they are mistreated, particularly when it comes to taxes. There seem to be reasons built into the system.

According to the 1977 Internal Revenue Service tax table a single adult pays a larger portion of taxes on his or her adjusted gross income. A single parent who has two teen-age sons at home and who makes $15,000 adjusted gross income would pay $507 more in taxes than would a married couple with a baby and the same income.

Such inequities in tax law go back to 1913, when the first federal income tax laws were passed. Then only couples from states where, by law, each spouse owned one half of the couple's property and income were able to divide their tax bill and pay at a lower overall rate. By 1948, Congress had changed the law so that couples in all states could split their family income and obtain the tax advantage. Such a policy did not take into account such factors as the number of single people who support aged parents or other family members. In 1948, singles were paying as much as forty-one percent more federal income tax than marrieds, on identical income. Vivien Kellems, an unmarried Connecticut Yankee, that year began her relentless, one-woman battle against the Internal Revenue Service. Finally Congress enacted the Tax Reform Act—but not until 1969! The tax was reduced, but singles are still taxed as much as twenty percent higher than married people.

On top of a federal income tax system that discriminates against singles, our country has a welfare system that holds many single women in its web.

The low salaries paid most women and the difficulty and expense in locating child care is leading many divorcées and widows to the conclusion that working is not worthwhile. Instead, they are turning to the welfare rolls. Of the nation's 2.5 million families receiving aid to families with dependent children, more than 80 percent are headed by women.

Husbandless mothers also are running into trouble in making such "normal" financial arrangements as getting credit cards, buying a house or a car, or even insuring the car—as required by law in many states.[27]

Single women frequently are unable to establish credit. Some widows have left credit accounts in their husband's name, even though the husband is dead.

For divorced women, economic problems can begin when the marriage breaks up. It may come through ill-advised legal help. Many lawyers who handle divorces are not experts in the tax field. Their main job is to advise clients of their rights under the law and to negotiate the best property settlement possible. Many overlook some of the tax effects upon the broken family following the divorce decree. For example, under present income tax standards, alimony is tax deductible for the husband and must be declared as taxable income for the wife. Child support, on the other hand, is neither. If the separation agreement doesn't specify what amount goes to child support, the entire payment is treated as alimony, a benefit for the man, but a road to heavier taxes for the woman. The parent who has custody of the child the greater part of the year generally is able to claim the child as a deduction on his or her tax return. The other parent may get the deduction if: (1) he or she contributed at least $600 toward support and the separation agreement gives him or her the deduction in writing; or (2) he or she contributed at least $1,200 for each child claimed and the other parent can't prove he or she contributed more.

Just because a divorce agreement states what financial support the wife will receive doesn't guarantee it will be paid, however. Roughly one half of all divorced women find that the promised alimony or child-support payments don't arrive. One study of fathers ordered to pay child support in a metropolitan county in Wisconsin found that "in the first year 42 percent made no payments at all and 20 percent were in arrears. By the sixth year, 71 percent were ignoring their obligations. Even more default on alimony."[28]

Elderly singles face special problems. Living on a set income, many are unable to meet rising costs or unexpected setbacks.

Many single people feel further caught in the grasp of the system because of laws that limit them from receiving government support under certain circumstances. For example:

> Provisions of the Aid to Dependent Children plan which calls for the withdrawal of funds if there is a man in the home, and Social Security provisions which cut off the retirement funds of widows who remarry are both examples of the injustices that now prevail, and that frustrate the possibility of productive relationships for some single persons.[29]

Economic problems tend to be most severe for divorced and widowed women of any age who have never worked at all. Many who had been "homemakers" during the years of a marriage find they were ill-prepared to enter the job market when the demand arose.

Those who do find jobs and a reasonable income still face financial concerns. Susan Jacoby notes that even when they make substantial salaries, many single women are less likely than men to make the kinds of financial investments that would assure their future economic security and independence. "Women aren't brought up to think about managing money alone."[30]

The church could be of better service to single adults by developing more practical ways for singles to discuss their financial concerns. Mixed with a sound theology of financial stewardship could be seminars, lectures, sessions on investment, legal guidelines, and sound financial planning. The church could help promote financial advocacy to help get some of the present laws changed which discriminate against single people. It could offer guidance on financial matters to persons facing divorce, widowhood, single parenting, by possibly utilizing the resources of laypersons who work in the financial and legal counseling fields. Through some creative planning the church could provide a very practical service to single persons who are struggling for financial security against a system that has not demonstrated its awareness of their plight.

FINDING A VALUE SYSTEM THAT WORKS

Bucking the Culture

In choosing not to be married, many single adults today must select alternative life-styles that clash with traditional value systems of the culture. In a culture that is marriage- and family-oriented, the single adult seeks to develop an integrated system of beliefs and values. This is not easy.

There are personal "tapes" which must be sorted out. Most of us have been "programmed" to accept marriage as the norm. The nuclear family has been portrayed as the model to be followed. Most of our value systems were shaped within such a context.

When a person chooses not to marry, or is thrown into sudden singleness by divorce, desertion, or death, then another value system must be adopted. Such matters as whether to (re)marry, questions about pre- and post-marital sex, abortion, masturbation, etc., must be faced. The extent of relationships with the opposite and the same sex take on a new appearance. Whether to live alone, in a commune, in an extended family, with parents, or with a lover must be considered.

For some it may mean a reintegration of a personal world view or a breakdown of a traditional value system. The single needs time, space, and support in being able to sort out, to reevaluate, and to restructure. To find a way to integrate personal views with traditional models is not easy, particularly if traditional views are the only ones accepted by family, the church, or closest friends.

To what extent should the culture be pressed to alter its view? Should traditional stances be reexamined and reinterpreted in the light of the new conditions we face, not necessarily to change, but to update, to deal more compassionately with the people who are being ground up in the clash? Who should be called upon to help? How can the church help to bring about change in thinking and life-style? Is the church too caught up in preserving the traditional viewpoint that it cannot, or will not, risk? What is the church's role as advocate for life-style, legal, and economic changes? What is its role as reconciler when value systems clash? Such questions are not easily answered. Some of the traditional "answers" may no longer fit. Many single adults who are wrestling to find a value system that works for them and still has integrity with the Christian faith wonder what the role of the church will be in that quest.

Obviously, the questions raised above are vast and complicated. Many of them only lead to other questions. It is not possible in this book to explore or address all of them. Two areas that need to be addressed, however, are sexuality and the relationship between commitment and marriage.

Sexuality and the Single Person

In 1970, the report on *Sexuality and the Human Community*, published by The United Presbyterian Church U.S.A., included a section on single adult persons. The report noted that "the style of Christian reflection on the ethics of sex which relies for its method on an understanding of the 'orders of creation' has resulted in marriage and the family becoming the model for ordering all sexual activity." It goes on to add:

> Nowhere is this more obvious than in the paucity of ethical guidance the church has to offer the single adult person. Our standards and teachings about premarital sex conduct assume that the practices and restraints which are being recommended are justifiable in terms of their value in preparing the couple for successful adjustment to marriage. But what of the person who never marries, or who having been married, is once again single? The conventions of society and those of the church both suggest that such a person must continue in or revert to the standards of conduct appropriate to those who are preparing for marriage.
>
> The inadequacy of this approach as a source of positive guidance and mature understanding of sexual behavior for the single adult should be obvious.[31]

Celibacy has been the traditional Biblical and historical alternative to marriage. Many adults who are single voluntarily adhere to celibacy as a valid option either to marriage or to sexual intercourse apart from marriage. Terri Williams writes in *Christianity Today* about her commitment as a Christian to the celibate style. She contends that "celibacy in no way implies withdrawal from people or a life of seclusion. In fact, one of the positive attractions of celibacy is that the single person has fewer continuing responsibilities, he is freer to give to those around him who need his love and help."[32] Ms. Williams goes on to suggest that Paul's encouragement to Christian celibacy in I Cor., ch. 7, is not a call to seclusion but to intensified involvement with persons who are in need. She does admit, however,

> that Paul is careful to say that celibacy is not for everyone. Although he considers it the better state (v. 38) and he believes people would probably be happier in it (v. 40), he realizes that personal needs (vs. 1–9) or needs of others (vs. 36–38) may

necessitate marriage. But it is clear that marriage, as such, ought not be the goal for the Christian. Marriage is proper and good, but it is not the goal.[33]

The *Sexuality and the Human Community* report recognizes that not all singles are satisfied with celibacy as the only way to address the questions concerning their sexuality. While affirming celibacy it notes that "celibacy is a valid option for those who adopt it voluntarily. Yet we question whether society has the right to impose celibacy or celibate standards on those who do not choose them."[34] The report suggests that the church has been of very little help as a source of positive guidance and mature understanding of sexual behavior for the single adult. As the single adult portion of the population increases, the questions and issues grow in complexity. Some of those people have made vocational decisions that preclude marriage. Others have hung back from the permanence of the marriage relationship out of fear or lack of self-confidence in heterosexual relationships. Some who choose not to marry are homosexual. Many are simply the victims of circumstance. These plus the variety of previously married single adults form a significantly large minority of adults who are "the victims of a 'conspiracy of silence' in the church concerning any positive and realistic ethical guidance for their lives."[35]

Since receiving that report in 1970, the church has continued to wrestle with some of the questions of human sexuality. Many of these questions have been limited in scope, however. The most recent concern over the ordination of homosexuals to the ministry has not yet been resolved. Linda LeSourd, writing in *It's O.K. to Be Single*, observes:

There is a danger of the Christian fellowship becoming so sanctimonious that those with deep unresolved problems are frightened into silence or hypocrisy. This is especially true in the area of sex. Some singles find it very difficult to handle the lack of sexual fulfillment; others suffer aftereffects of our warped cultural attitudes toward sex; still others are badly misinformed with regard to sexual matters; and many are heavily burdened with feelings of guilt. A significant number of seemingly innocent Christian women wrestle with problems of homosexuality, immorality, rape and sexual molestation. The church has a responsibility to minister forgiveness, new life and healing.[36]

The church's renewed interest in helping people deal with sexuality seldom focuses on the single person. Fortunately, the church has turned from denouncing all sexuality as earthly and evil and begun to affirm it as an aspect of God's goodness.

One of the important conclusions we draw from God's revelation in Christ is that our sexuality is an instrument of God's reconciling activity. The God who could overcome our alienation from himself and from each other has invested human sexuality with far more than procreative significance. It is truly a vehicle of the spirit and a means of human communion. It is also true that our sexual endowments can be, and often are, turned to self-serving and uncharitable purposes. Thus, sexual gestures are not intrinsically moral or immoral. They derive their moral significance from the reconciling or the alienating purposes they serve.[37]

This kind of affirmation of sexuality, and a realization that it can be an instrument of both human sinfulness and God's grace, is not totally conveyed by the church to our society. What many singles experience from religious leaders is an attitude that sexuality, particularly sexual intercourse, is to be totally confined to marriage. And many of these leaders seem to assume that everyone will marry. Those who do not marry are urged to be celibate, to practice sublimation, or be condemned as immoral. To offer a pat cliché, "God is sufficient," may not take seriously the intensity of the dilemma the single adult faces.

Many previously married single women struggle to find an adequate sexual ethic. Returning to single life after years of marriage, they find the new morality at once incomprehensible and threatening. They get caught in a double bind: whereas earlier generations of women were taught that sexual appetites were part of male functioning, not female, they are now aware that sexual drives are natural. At the same time, they are still caught in a culture that permits men casual sexual encounters but requires deep emotional commitments from women. A variety of sexual experience has been traditionally available to men and denied to women—or at least "good women."

The concerns are strong. Singles today find themselves in a variety of situations for which there are no trite answers that seem to fit. Some of the common problem areas are: What does a person do with a strong sexual attraction that doesn't involve a love relationship? What about "one night stands"? What does a woman do with a man who wants to go to bed with her after the first date? What should be done when there are strong sexual attractions on the part of both parties but a commitment to marriage is not present or feasible at the time?

Countless people in our society struggle for an understanding of their sexuality. Sex so often gets entangled with stressful personality needs, having little to do with the direct communication of love and affection. People misuse it for instant intimacy, thinking it can solve all their relational problems. They misuse sex for reassurance, self-esteem, as an expression of anger and hostility, and as a weapon.

Masturbation is an issue with which many singles struggle. What does a single do with sexual drives when there is no close relationship with another person? Masturbation is often an unspoken outlet. Kinsey's reports showed that ninety-two percent of the total adult male population masturbated. The report also showed that the unmarried masturbate more frequently than married people. In discussing female masturbation, Edwards and Hoover report:

> The pattern seems to be that women who remain single tend to continue masturbation throughout their lives, while older women whose husbands are in failing health, or who are widowed or divorced, resume or increase their masturbation practice as time goes on.[38]

Both Judaism and Christianity have generally rejected masturbation, insisting that any form of sexual activity should be for the purpose of reproduction alone. For many centuries, it was considered to be the first cardinal sin by the medieval church, outranking both fornication and adultery. At times in Jewish history it was punished by death.

Medical myths about the consequences of masturbation (i.e., diminished intelligence, aggravated acne, impotence in normal intercourse) have long been dispelled.

> There is nearly unanimous medical opinion that no physical harm to the body is produced even by frequent masturbation. There is even some argument for the positive values of masturbation in relieving sexual tension and attendant physical discomfort in the pelvic region, in contributing to psychosexual development, and in providing a satisfactory alternative form of sexual gratification to single persons or to married persons during periods of separation where intercourse would be inappropriate or impossible.[39]

The *Sexuality and the Human Community* report goes on to urge:

> Since masturbation is often one of the earliest pleasurable sexual experiences which is identifiably genital, we consider it essential that the church, through its teachings and through the attitudes it encourages in Christian homes, contribute to a healthy under-

standing of this experience which will be free of guilt and shame. The ethical significance of masturbation depends entirely on the context in which it takes place.[40]

Such a position on a traditionally taboo subject indicates that the church is becoming more cognizant of the theological, psychological, medical, and social interrelationships that surround most questions of human sexuality. Many practices that have been previously condemned are being seen in a new light. Social situations have altered perspectives considerably on many issues. For single adults this may give rising hope that the church will develop an approach to human sexuality that is more sensitive to their needs.

Nancy Hardesty suggests some guidelines for such an approach:

> Our theology of sexuality must be based on a model of personhood rather than of marriage; it must apply as fully to the single person as to the married. Our ethical thinking . . . must include the single adult in addition to adolescents, engaged couples and married persons.[41]

What About Commitment and Marriage?

One of the recurring questions the single adult must address is the matter of commitment and marriage. The pairing pressure and the nuclear family ideal do not let up for most singles.

Of the single adults I surveyed, 82.9 percent indicated that they had previously been married. When asked if they expected to marry, 41.2 percent said yes, 24.1 indicated no, and 20.4 percent checked maybe. The largest percentage of singles do expect to (re)marry. Statistics indicate that three out of four divorced persons do eventually remarry.[42]

Counselors who have worked with singles who are facing the possibility of (re)marriage indicate four basic groupings:

1. Singles who wish to get married as a matter of preference. These people may dream, even fantasize about marriage, but they survive if they don't and refuse to lose the benefits of living because they are not married. Ultimately, they resolve the issue of their status and are at peace. The church often is greatly benefited by these people. Too little is known about happy singles!

2. Singles who will get married at any cost. They force themselves to accept mates who may be significantly different in culture and conduct in order to get married. Some even sacrifice morals and integrity in order to ingratiate themselves and gain marriage. What often follows for many of these people is unhappiness, disillusionment, and an increased sense of failure.

3. Singles who are determined to remain single. For many, their unmarried status is fulfilling and happy.

4. Singles who determine to remain single because of their dislike or distrust of the opposite sex.[43]

The question of commitment and marriage is, for many single adults, not an easy one to make. Some fear making any lasting commitments to persons of the opposite sex. Possibly they were emotionally scarred over a divorce or desertion. Others, who have not been married, fear making commitments toward marriage because of their suspicion of the institution of marriage. Others simply "don't want to be tied down."

Many singles are suspicious of the current form of marriage, as it centers around the nuclear family unit. Anthropologist Ashley Montagu strongly charges that "the American nuclear family—a husband, wife, and one or more children—is a social unit which systematically produces mental illness in its members."[44]

Increased self-awareness of women has resulted in a growing disaffection with marriage and its role system. This, in turn, has altered the point of view of many men, who have to reevaluate their own role attitudes about marriage.

Some people entered marriage too hastily and, when the marriage relationship didn't work, realized they needed to work out some personal growth needs. Carole Klein reflects, in speaking about previously married middle-aged women:

> Fear of independence led them to make a dependent relationship that choked off their personal identities. Through the years they gave back to their husbands the images their husbands wanted to see, and now when they look in their own mirrors, they see a stranger.
>
> Identity crises are common among middle-aged women, and it has less to do with menopause and "empty nests" than it does with the terrible knowledge that they have spent a lifetime in separation from themselves.[45]

Many women see such marriages as a substitute to their personal growth. Building a secure single person identity, then, is an important matter to them. "People who study marriage," writes Carole Klein, "feel that more and more women are frustrated by an image of themselves as narrowly home-centered. They feel, too, that the choice *not* to marry relates to the rising awareness that in marriage there must be room for two independent people of multiple interests."[46] She continues:

> The major change that confronts marriage is that many people no longer feel they need it, and certainly do not need it in its older forms. Among the dusty old ideas that are being cleared out of tradition's attic is the idea that there is only one way to live as a family.[47]

Today many people are experimenting with alternative styles of familial living. Communal and extended family arrangements increased since the early '60s, largely as an attempt to explore new alternatives. However, many persons who experienced such arrangements found that either they, or others in the situation, could not handle the dynamics. Some arrangements worked well as an alternative to the nuclear family. Like marriage, however, some people found that, in any arrangement of close living, personal self-understanding and integrity are necessary ingredients.

A secure single-person identity is crucial as any person thinks through the nature of commitment and relationship with others. In writing about the importance of working through grief following a divorce, Krantzler emphasizes that it can be the beginning of a journey of self-discovery.

> If during the mourning process you are able to get in touch with your feelings and from them build a secure, single person identity, you set the stage for a re-evaluation of every part of your life: your moral and ethical standards, your occupational goals, relations with your children and friends, and your style of life.
>
> One of the best indications of such a commitment is your willingness to risk new relationships with the opposite sex.[48]

Lyon holds that "all but a few single persons want more intimacy and continuity of interpersonal relationships."[49] Remarriage, for some, is seen as an avenue for such intimacy. Yet, a hasty remarriage can be a major impediment to sustained personal growth. Most divorce lawyers counsel clients not to rush into another marriage. Krantzler writes:

> Men and women who do rush into another marriage are usually those who have gotten stuck at some point in the mourning process. They still think of themselves as half-persons. They cry out, "I need someone to belong to," when they should be exploring the question, "Who do I belong with?"
>
> Just as destructive, though not so prevalent, is the decision to swear off marriage completely, taken by people whose fear of future pain is so intense that they vow never again to expose themselves to the risks of closeness.[50]

The church could help singles who are facing such questions by providing small-group support systems, personal counseling opportunities with people who are willing to listen and offer constructive guidance when it is sought. Rebuilding a healthy view of oneself, and of marriage, as well as of singleness, is often a slow process.

If a single person does find another person with whom commitment is a possibility, then the question of living together has to be addressed. Cohabitation apart from marriage is increasing among single persons. Of those I have counseled for marriage over the past five years, nearly thirty percent indicated that they were living together.

My experience seems supported by research figures. In a survey of 1,099 Penn State University students responding to the question "Are you now living with, or have you ever lived with, someone of the opposite sex?" a total of 360, or 32.8 percent, responded in the affirmative. Figures were nearly identical for both men and women.[51]

There are many kinds of living together arrangements (known in some circles as LTAs).

> Perhaps most common are the courtship unions of young people who move in together with an understanding that perhaps they will eventually marry. There are LTAs in which both partners seem to be flaunting their life-style as a sign of social liberation. These are often brief. Then there are the frankly manipulative relationships in which a woman (or a man) is kept in exchange for sexual favors, or to perform as a socially acceptable consort at public appearances.[52]

The first category is no longer limited to young people. More and more persons who were previously married seem to want "to make sure" before they make a commitment to remarry.

Edwards and Hoover point out two motivations that lead people to live together.

In the first place, one or both of the parties usually believe they are in love and they want to be together to satisfy the strong emotional hunger they feel. In addition, there is almost always a strong sexual attraction and a desire for an exclusive relationship.[53]

Some single people, particularly those who have been previously married, want to test their commitment in stages. They have enjoyed the "falling in love with love" experience, but are a bit reluctant to see this as a guarantee of foreverness. Marriage expectations center more on a desire for a deep and open emotional commitment and less on parenthood, status, and economic security. Living together is seen as one way to test that potential. This does not require the promises of a commitment beyond what they are prepared to give.

Many authors and counselors warn of dangers and complications in cohabiting. Such warnings are often found in popular magazines, possibly so they can be heard or read by persons involved. In "Living Together Is a Rotten Idea," author Judith Krantz warns her readers:

> Living together, except in the rarest cases, is always a half-way measure; it is not a true commitment (self-serving statements by men to the contrary), not the sink or swim of marriage, but a mere dog paddle at the shallow end of the pool.[54]

Likewise, Karen Durbin, writing in *Harper's Magazine*, says:

> Living together, even though it involves no light decision, is not the commitment that marriage is. No matter how much you think you love each other, how limitless the future may seem to both of you, you still haven't called in the neighbors for a house raising. Living together remains an essentially private arrangement, unintegrated into any structure outside that of shared emotions.
>
> Living together is essentially tentative; inevitably, there is a quality of experiment about it.[55]

There are many possible complications to living together besides the tentativeness of the situation. Complications can be psychological, as well as economic and legal. There are many of the restrictions of being married, but few of the advantages: lower income taxes, insurance rates, better chance for jobs and promotions, as well as a number of legal protections. Since very few states recognize common-law marriages, if a cohabiting partner dies, there are no community property rights. Coping with guilt may not be easy for the couple who is living under such arrangements. Possible rejection by family may be a growing fear. Conflicts with one's religious background may surface.

Yet many single people are choosing to live together today. Those who wish to minister to such people must not simply reject the arrangement as immoral. There may be some situations for which living together is valid. For instance, many senior adults have found such an arrangement more economically advantageous than getting married and losing Social Security benefits.

To find a value system that works is not easy for the single adult. Different values conflict with one another in such a culture. Some premises that the church has strongly adhered to in the past may need to be set aside in order to deal with the single adult in a way that demonstrates the care and compassion of Jesus Christ.

SUMMARY

The world of the single adult is complicated. Singles have a variety of needs and concerns. Some of these are unique to the single. While our society has stereotyped "singles" and drawn conclusions which may not be valid, the world of the single continues to demand responses and pose problems which are intense.

The church is in a position to provide a valuable ministry to single persons. To do so, however, demands an openness and a sensitivity on the part of church people.

We need to look carefully at the "message" that is being conveyed to single persons through our language and style. While a ministry to married persons and families is important, there are single persons in our churches and communities who need to be heard and cared for. Providing competent counseling, as well as opportunities to share feelings and experiences with people who have gone through similar struggles in facing singleness, would indicate the church's concern for wholeness and healing. Explorations into the meaning of marriage and possible Christian alternatives to marriage, as well as a sensitive and realistic sex ethic, might assist people who are trying to live within our system as single people.

The church needs to come to grips with the variety of types of singles, helping them to cope with their unique needs and concerns, and to channel their gifts and strengths. The development of a Biblical understanding of singleness would be a valuable affirmation of singles. Then, finding the most appropriate ways to minister to the singles in our churches and community would show that the church really does intend to carry on a ministry of liberation and healing to all persons, including the single adult.

4

SINGLES ARE SWINGERS

(GETTING BEYOND STEREOTYPES
TO PARTICULAR NEEDS)

NUMEROUS STEREOTYPES regarding single adults abound. Susan Jacoby notes:

> Like any newly discovered minority, singles tend to be viewed by the majority in misleading, monolithic terms. Stereotypes about the unmarried frequently seem as ludicrous as the image of a black population with a universal sense of rhythm and love for watermelon. . . . Single men and women in different areas of the country express a combination of dismay, resentment, and amusement when they are asked about their public image.[1]

Stereotypes can be used to make general remarks about a body of people. They help to classify. But they also can dehumanize and take away from the variety of giftedness that exists in any group. Stereotypes are generalities that are not accurate for most in a given body of persons. "Singles are swingers" is an example.

There are a variety of situations and conditions in which single adults may be found living within our society (Table 1).

Single persons are individuals living in every conceivable combination in Table 1, with varying degrees of adjustment from miserable to content.

For instance, a young adult may be living with a roommate because he or she is divorced and a full-time parent. Or, a

TABLE 1

COMBINATIONS OF SINGLE ADULT SETTINGS

Age	Proximity to Others	Marital Status		Parental Status
Young	Living alone	Never married— uninvolved		No children
Mid-life	Living roommate	Casual relations— intimate, but not romantic		A need for children
Older	Living lover/spouse	Coupled	Separated	Full-time parent
Elderly	Living with family	Married	Divorced	Part-time parent
	Living in community		Widowed	Barred from children
				Children grown

mid-life person may be living with a lover, separated, and barred from seeing his children. Or, two elderly people may live together, both widowed, the children grown, but they may choose not to get married for fear of losing pension benefits. Or, a mid-life adult, living alone, never-married, may wish to have children. There are many combinations of single adulthood existing in our complex society.

Each combination of singleness has its own special feelings, unique to the circumstance. These may be determined by age, sex, financial condition and, of course, whether the person has always been single or has recently entered the single state. For example, the never-married frequently see themselves as different from the formerly married. Often they will not even date singles in categories different from their own. Some fear that they will not be understood. The formerly married sometimes feel that they would be uncomfortable with someone who had never been married.

Similarly, the widowed, separated from their spouses by death, sometimes believe that their feelings cannot possibly be understood by the divorced, many of whom deliberately severed their marital bonds. The widowed frequently feel that they would have even less in common with never-married singles. The separated person may be isolated from all of these.

Basically, single adults can be grouped in four categories of singleness: never-married, separated, divorced, and widowed. Within each of these there may be any number of the combinations previously mentioned. In addition, the young single adult and the single parent need to be considered.

The Adult Who Has Never Married

Adults who have never married may be single by choice or by circumstance. Because they have never married, they may well expect to be interrogated on the subject many times.

."How come you're not married? What have you got against marriage?"

"Do you think there's something wrong with you?"

"Did you never meet the right person?"

"Did the right person get away?"

"Don't you want the responsibility of children?"

"Are you having too much fun to get married?"

"How long do you plan to stay single?"

The list goes on. Those who haven't been married must learn to cope with all manner of insinuations about their singleness. Many do, while others find it vexing and difficult.

Carol was young and single. She had a serious relationship with another first-year student. When he left college the relationship ended. She dated several others in the remainder of the term, but nothing on the serious side. After graduation, she taught fourth grade. Marriage was not a priority for her as she began a career. Occasionally, when she expressed this attitude, the impression she received was that she was odd.

The notion that one is not "normal" unless married can hit and hurt hard. Parental pressure, the myth that there is a "right person" for everyone, and the image of wholeness linked with marriage have an impact on the unmarried person. With these messages often comes a tendency to devalue one's worth. As Edwards and Hoover note:

> Like any group that has been constantly ignored or downgraded, singles come to believe what others say about them. And even though they may not acknowledge it consciously, they behave as if they believe it by limiting the scope of their existence, by not taking chances in their personal and work lives, by not really choosing when they have the opportunity, and by seeing themselves as only temporary people, not rooted firmly in the present.
>
> Sometimes this self-devaluing hits singles at significant times later in life when they least expect it.[2]

Many singles have convinced themselves that their reasons for not marrying in their younger years were valid. Then they realize that they are getting older, the right person didn't come along, and still hasn't appeared on the scene, and probably won't. At such a point their self-image falls. As one single woman in her forties admitted, while in a despondent mood: "I feel so temporary. I have this gnawing feeling that I've missed the boat and it makes me feel like only half a person."

Yet, there are also some positive indications that adults who have never married are coping quite well with their singleness. The sheer size of this group makes it a factor to be reckoned with.

Susan Jacoby[3] notes that the adults who have never married jumped from an estimated 12.9 million in 1960 to 16.2 million in 1970. The under twenty-five age group accounted for the largest share of that growth. She indicates that the post-World War II baby boom was a predictable factor in the singles increase of the mid-'60s. An even more important factor included adults who chose later marriage, a spiraling divorce rate, and a marked trend against early remarriage after divorce.

Gail Sheehy writes in *Passages*[4] that roughly ten percent of American women never marry, while only five percent of American men over forty years of age are unmarried. She compares statistics on how single men and women make it through their status of singleness. "By all accounts of statistics and studies, men need marriage more than women do."[5] Older men, in particular, seem to be at a loss to find purpose apart from marriage. This is particularly true when they begin to get devalued in their job. For many men, the job often is the source of meaning.

> Between the ages of 25 and 34, there is not a great deal of difference in education, occupation, or income between the single men and single women. But by the time they reach middle age, 46 to 54, the distance between them has stretched to a gulf. The single women are more educated, have higher average incomes, and work in more prestigious occupations. And it is not the old maid but the old bachelor who suffers from the poorest showing of psychological distress.[6]

Unfortunately our culture has produced many unliberated men who are unable to cope with such distress. Many suffer from what Warren Farrell describes as "emotional constipation." In an atmosphere of business life, which frequently tends to dehumanize, "men cannot help but be either emotionally incompetent (unable to handle emotions expressed by others) or emotionally constipated (unable to express their own emotions) or both."[7]

Single as well as married men in our society suffer from such a hesitancy to work through psychological distress. Many lack the freedom to express emotion, to admit personal stress, and to break dependency on success, money, and status. Many have bought into a life-style that is void of much meaning except through job status, sexual supremacy, and affluent spending.

Women, on the other hand, seem to be freer to respond to consciousness-raising opportunities and personal growth groups, and to explore new dimensions of single life. The women's liberation movement has brought about a good deal of this new direction. Opportunities for sharing personal experiences and dilemmas evoke response by more women than men. Women seem freer than men to face seriously the meaning of their singleness.

A larger percentage of women than men participate in singles groups. Women seem more willing to explore and utilize such opportunities. How to reach never-married men remains a challenge in most communities and churches.

Many unmarried persons have learned to explore new options for directing their interests and energies. Some choose their profession as an outlet. For women, that outlet may frequently be through what is described as a paranurturing profession. As social workers, teaching nuns, custodians of the orphaned and retarded, many single women care for the children who are lacking the advantages of stable homes. Still others flock to metropolitan areas devoting their lives to the care of public men and politicians. Some, like Rosemary Woods, do so to the exclusion of any other deep personal tie. Still others, primarily the younger singles, find office jobs in the city. Some of these want the freedom to move about.

> These are the women who choose in the twenties to keep their options open. Yet by the very choice of impermanence, like the transient men, they do follow a pattern—the pattern of prolonged wandering without commitments.[8]

This impermanence is often spoken of as a cause of frustration among those who work with single adults.

In a society where the institution of marriage is being tested and reshaped, many men and women are hesitant to make the commitment to marry. Previously marriage and family met the needs in most people's lives; today many singles find that those patterns are changing.

> We have a society with far different economic and social realities than have ever existed before, and there is no longer unanimity about the need for, or the ability of, marriage and childbearing to provide fulfillment for the individual or for society.[9]

If the never-married person is going to face singleness with hope and fulfillment, it is crucial to work out a positive vision of the single life. More and more singles are beginning to discover the advantages of single life on a deeper basis. They are making discoveries about self-identity and seeing singlehood as a unique opportunity to explore the possibilities of meaningful work, freedom, love, and caring relationships in a new way. For many, the search for self-identity rates above the quest for a mate.

One of the challenges facing all single people is to work through to a positive understanding and outlet for one's sexuality. This is particularly true for the never-married person. With the sexual revolution and its effects, there are countless styles being experienced by single adults. Some choose to be heterosexually active, while homosexuals and lesbians seem to be finding more open expression. This trend has produced both awareness and conflict within church and society in recent years. Some singles have chosen celibacy as a valid direction for their single life. The choices seem to be many for the never-married. Not all of these, of course, are personally satisfying, nor all equally conducive to a positive self-image for each single person.

The church can be of help to the person who has never married by being sensitive to the issues, and aiding such a person or persons to work toward a positive vision of their singleness. Parental pressures for marriage, feelings of loneliness, questions about sexual standards, and finding positive outlets for dating and friendship are some of the needs commonly expressed by the never-marrieds. Men, particularly, need to develop a self-image and life-style that is positive and satisfying. Caring friendships with people of both sexes, who can be trusted, are most frequently sought. To help both men and women who have never married to channel their interests and concerns toward human need is an open challenge to the church.

The Adult Who Is Single by Separation

Separation may be one of the stages of singleness which is most difficult to describe or understand. The adult who is separated is, in many ways, caught between two worlds. While still being legally married the person may be emotionally divorced, or the person may be separated but still emotionally carrying the scars or hurts from that separation. Edwards and Hoover describe the separated person as in a state of ambivalence. As one separated man remarked: "I feel like I'm poison. I'm not really married and not really free."

Such a state of ambivalence expresses itself in a variety of ways for the separated person. He or she may be caught in vacillating emotions about marriage and divorce. There may be questions of whether or not there is still a chance to save the marriage. Pressure from friends or relatives may further complicate those feelings. A person may experience feelings of guilt over the separation, especially if he or she was the one to make the decision. There are tense questions over finances between two households.

For some couples, the decision to separate is a way of avoiding the pain of divorce. For others, the decision to divorce may have been made by one or both persons, but they are afraid to admit it. Some may be trying "a trial separation," hoping that the time apart will help bridge the distance between them. Some may seek professional counseling during the separation, others may want it but not know where to turn to get it, and still others are afraid to seek help. Frequently, one party is willing to seek counseling, while the other is not.

The ambivalence of continued indecision may find its outlet through emotional distress, as well as through such physical symptoms as insomnia, severe fatigue, headaches, weight loss, or gastrointestinal upsets. An ambivalent state can be a very stressful time.

The person who is separated experiences this new state as an awkward and difficult time. There may be some feeling of relief especially if the marriage relationship was stormy or tense. If one parent has the children, that person may feel "caught" in a child's world. The parent without the children may be experiencing times of loneliness, anger, and guilt over not being able to be with the children. Times with the children can become expensive and demanding.

Social life may add to the strain, especially when one tries to maintain a relationship with mutual friends (who are usually coupled). One may find such friends backing away, out of their own feelings of awkwardness. Often a marital separation is a threat to them, especially if their own marriage has been shaky. Some stay away, fearing an effect upon their own marital relationship. The separated person may begin to experience feelings of alienation and rejection. Loneliness is a common feeling experienced during this time. This may be intensified at special holidays or on weekends, when memories arise of times with strong emotional content, and when one has extended time alone.

Some couples never get to the point of making a clean decision. They want their freedom, yet may want to be "safe" to return if possible. "By being separated, one can continue to have some of the benefits of being married—for example, a better deal on income taxes, credit ratings, and job promotions —how it works out emotionally is often another matter."[10]

Yet, until a clean break or a decision to reconcile is made, neither person can begin to build a future in constructive ways.

> Probably the greatest kindness the separated can do for themselves is to make the decision—either get back with their spouse and declare themselves married (even though the marriage may be far from what they'd like it to be) or make a break, go through the divorce, and declare themselves single. Only then, realistically, can they begin to launch a new life.[11]

Separation also exists for those marriages where one or both persons are in the military, or have jobs that require travel for long periods of time. The couple may be married but experience an emotional and physical separation which puts a heavy strain on the marriage.

Separated persons can be helped by having people who will provide understanding and support. A caring community can provide an outlet for venting and sorting out feelings and exploring alternatives in the decision-making process. Certainly, competent guidance regarding divorce is necessary before the actual act of filing is taken.

THE ADULT WHO IS SINGLE BY DIVORCE

Divorce has become an increasing reality in American society. The 5.9 million divorced adults comprise one of the highest divorce rates in the world. Our 3.72 divorces per 1,000 population in 1972 was higher than that of Cuba (3.23 per 1,000) and Russia (2.64 per 1,000). That rate climbed to 4.4 per 1,000 in 1973 and 4.5 divorces per 1,000 during the twelve months ending in August 1974.[12] There was an 80 percent divorce rate increase between 1960 and 1972. A less noticed phenomenon is the growing reluctance of divorced men and women to leap into early second marriages. By 1970, there were more than 1.3 million divorced people under thirty-five years of age who had not remarried. This is double the 1960 figure.[13]

Edwards and Hoover cite that currently about one half of all single women have been married before. They also note that once a woman is divorced or widowed, she is in no big rush to remarry. They relate 1970 U.S. Census statistics which show that more than one third more divorced women than men had *not* remarried at the time of the census.[14]

Glick also cites the 1970 Census figures to point out that the proportion of divorced (and not remarried) continued to be lower among men approaching middle age (thirty-five to forty-four years of age) than among women of comparable age. The proportion was 3.6 to 5.5 percent. Education and profession seem to be contributing factors. Women who have the most education and the higher income are less likely to marry or to continue in marriage. Those with lesser achievement in their education background and work experience are more likely to marry. Statistics seem to demonstrate that the most lasting marriages are contracted by men in upper socio-economic levels. He lists as some possible reasons for this trend five factors:

1. An increasing proportion of young wives with small families who have succeeded in translating their higher education into jobs that make them financially independent of their husbands.
2. An increasing proportion of couples whose income has risen to a level at which they can afford the cost of obtaining a divorce to resolve a marriage that is not viable or working well.
3. Increased availability of free legal aid which may have per-

mitted larger numbers of impoverished or lower income
families to obtain divorce.

4. The effects of the war in Vietnam, which complicated the
   transition of millions of young men into marriage or else
   made their adjustment into marriage more difficult.

5. Greater social acceptance of divorce. In other words, a relaxa-
   tion of attitudes toward divorce by a growing number of
   religious denominations, reform of divorce laws, such as no-
   fault divorce.[15]

Adults caught in divorce are required to make a variety of
adjustments. Dr. Thomas Holmes, psychiatrist at the University of Washington, found that the three most stressful events
in life were: (1) the death of a spouse, (2) a divorce, and (3)
a marital separation. The effects of such stresses often lead to
major illnesses and are found to be more stressful than the
death of a close family member or even a long-term jail sen-
tence.[16]

In his book *Creative Divorce*, Krantzler approaches divorce
as a grief period that needs to be constructively dealt with and
worked through.

For many people, divorce marks the first time they have ever
really been single. Responding to the pairing pressure, many
rushed into marriage at an early age. Often those marriages
existed on dependency patterns. Divorced people are sometimes classified with those who are "single again." But in fact,
they may never have functioned as totally independent adults.
The new experience of finding oneself as "single" for the first
time can be devastating.

In a world of new situations, with none of the familiar
guideposts of married life, the divorced person has no choice
but to begin to behave as a separate person, not as half of a
couple. That may be a totally new adventure. Jim Smoke,
writing in *Growing Through Divorce*, describes the experience
this way:

All divorced persons must face the reality that they stand as one, not two. Many people stay in a marriage long after the love has gone just so they will not physically be alone.

Letting go in the physical area means slowly accepting the reality that the other person is not there any longer and will never be there again. Accepting this reality means accepting the hurt of being alone.[17]

Or, as Krantzler relates: "It is during times like these that separated or divorced people are shaken by how much of what they had thought was their independent identities had been bound up in their marital relationship."[18]

Krantzler describes how in his own experience of divorce, he went through

what all divorced people, men and women, go through to a greater or lesser degree—first, a recognition that a relationship had died. Then, a period of mourning, and finally, a slow, painful, emotional readjustment to the facts of single life.

I experienced the pitfalls along the way—the wallowing in self-pity, the refusal to let go of the old relationship, the repetition of old ways in relating to new people, the confusion of past emotions with present reality and I emerged the better for it.[19]

Divorce can force a person to come to grips with himself or herself in many new ways.

By coming to terms with ourselves as single people—by accepting the fact that living alone need not mean living lonely—we are laying the groundwork, if we so choose, for future relationships far more satisfying than the ones we left behind.[20]

The divorced person may be shocked at what must be faced during the stages of grief. Not only is there an awareness of suddenly being single, but that fact may be reinforced by old friends, business associates, or relatives.

It is often difficult for other people to face the divorce of a friend or relative. There is a tendency to identify a guilty party, to put the blame on someone. Sometimes that may be the case, which of course makes it easier to take sides. The "guilty party" is then left on the outside. Friends find it difficult to know how to relate to the divorced couple. Previously, they could relate to a couple. But the divorce changed that. In the awkwardness of trying to relate to a new entity, many "friends" simply avoid the divorced person as "a threat." This is a common experience of divorced women. Motives for socializing begin to be interpreted as "mate hunting." The new state of aloneness can be devastating for many people.

Social rejection is experienced in other ways. If a person is participating in the church, then he or she has to grapple with the position of the church in regard to divorce. Whatever the church's official position, the unofficial rejection of divorce frequently comes through. Divorce is sinful and a sign of failure.

As Smoke, himself out of a conservative theological approach, yet able to minister to a variety of single adult situations, states:

> In a religious community, divorce has stood for a long time as the somewhat unforgivable sin. The Bible does not teach this but the church has somehow convinced a lot of people that it does. Divorce often becomes a worse sin than stealing or murder. A divorced person is looked upon as permanently marred, bruised, tainted, or condemned. Although these viewpoints seem very medieval and un-Christlike, they are experienced by many people who have gone through a divorce.[21]

Krantzler says that divorce is a crisis that must be lived through. It can be "a new opportunity to improve on the past and create a fuller life—if you can come to terms with the past, recognize self-defeating behavior, and be willing to change it."[22]

Divorce often can involve feelings of grief. Definite stages need to be worked through. A relationship has ended, died.

There can be periods of mourning in which the death is recognized and accepted. Such acceptance can lead toward the rebirth of an independent single person.

Divorcing persons need a supportive group of people to help them in human and practical ways. That help may come by having someone who will listen without judging or condemning. It may come from someone who has gone through a similar trauma. It may come from a person knowledgeable in community resources, who can indicate where help can be obtained when help is needed.

Unfortunately, many divorced people get trapped at such points. When they are vulnerable it is easy to head in destructive directions. This is true in terms of seeking a new social world.

> A person's social existence is drastically altered by divorce. The divorced person no longer seems to fit the world of the married. Social contacts and social calendars change abruptly when people separate. A divorced person is tossed from the security of always having a special someone there to having no one there. If they intend to continue socializing in the human world they are forced to go out with members of the same sex or they are forced to go to bars, clubs and singles' groups and compete for the attention of members of the opposite sex. The singles' world can be a scary world and can send you running back to the security of your home or apartment. Little wonder that so many singles are in hiding.[23]

It is also at the point of vulnerability that divorced people jump right into the dating game and try quickly to establish a new relationship that leads to a new marriage. Propelled by their own insecurity or the fear of being alone, they rebound into another marriage. Krantzler suggests that "men and women who do rush into another marriage are usually those who have become stuck at some point in the mourning process.

They still think of themselves as half-persons. They cry out [either verbally, by action, or both], 'I need someone to belong to,' when they should be exploring the question, 'Who do I belong with?' "

On the other hand, the decision to swear off marriage completely can be just as destructive. It is often "taken by people whose fear of future pain is so intense that they vow never again to expose themselves to the risks of closeness."[24]

At the time of divorce, people can be helped to adjust to their divorce and the new demands it places upon them. Without such help it is easy to repeat their unhappy past with another bad relationship.

Both men and women seem to be emotionally devastated by divorce. Just as many men as women sleepwalk through a divorce right into a "new life" that is a glossed-over repetition of their past. Women may more readily seek out some new alternatives and sources of help, however.

> Women can seek help from friends, books, magazines, and professional counseling. Men are not supposed to need any help. As a result, men have developed even greater capacities than women for running away from their feelings and avoiding the opportunities for personal growth that a creative divorce offers.[25]

At the onset of a divorce or separation this may not appear to be true. Quite often it is the wife who seems to be overwhelmed, while the husband, to all external appearances, sails on smoothly. Society seems to accord men greater freedom to go out, meet new people, do things more readily. And the man still has his job. His strong-man facade can be kept up if he has hobbies—golf, fishing, spectator sports.

The trap comes in the flight from self. The man will work sixteen hours a day six days a week, then fill the seventh day with activity. Or, he can have an "eternal night on the town," jumping from bar to bar, woman to woman, party to party. When carried to excess, however, bachelorizing can become a means to avoid acknowledging real feelings and a trap that keeps a man from living in the present. Krantzler contends that if after a year and a half or two years, you were to plot the comparative rates of growth on the same chart, the woman's rate would proceed from an initial low to a high, while the man's would appear relatively horizontal—neither as initially low nor as ultimately high as the woman's.[26]

Divorced singles need to look squarely at the sources of guilt feelings, to compare systems of values against experience, and to begin to work through their divorced life as a time for creative growth. Many divorced people who are helped through such a process begin to develop a more creative outlet for their interests and pleasures.

The church can play a constructive part in this process if it chooses to do so. This demands that the church assess its position on divorce and its willingness to stand with the divorced person through any time of need.

The Presbyterian Church, until the first quarter of the twentieth century, stayed very close to what was regarded as the "Scriptural" basis of divorce. The two grounds for which it claimed to find some Biblical support were adultery and malicious desertion.[27] Yet, the Biblical view on divorce seems varied.

Divorce was taken for granted in the Old Testament. (See Lev. 21:7, 14; 22:13; Num. 30:9.) It was the traditional right of the husband to "put away his wife," as Abraham did with Hagar (Gen. 21:14). A "bill of divorcement" was to be prepared (see Isa. 50:1; Jer. 3:8), with a definite charge by the husband, and therefore presumably in the presence of some public official. It was formally presented to the woman for the divorce.

It was only natural that a divorcée be allowed to remarry,

though she was not to return to her former husband. Contrary to later Christian principles, this seemed to have closed the door on reconciliation.

In spite of later prohibitions against divorce (as in Mal. 2:13–16), and the stern attitude taken by many of the Jewish rabbis, divorce was a frequent occurrence. Ezra, ch. 9, encouraged it when there were mixed marriages. The early Mishnah allowed divorce for violation of the Law or of Jewish customs, such as the breaking of a vow, appearing in public with disheveled hair, or conversing indiscriminately with men. In a later period, the Talmud allowed a wife to claim a divorce in certain instances, for example, if her husband had a loathsome or communicable disease.

Jesus addressed the issue of divorce on a couple of different occasions. Matthew alone records his statement from the Sermon on the Mount:

> It was also said, "Whoever divorces his wife, let him give her a certificate of divorce." But I say to you that every one who divorces his wife, except on the ground of unchastity, makes her an adulteress; and whoever marries a divorced woman commits adultery. (Matt. 5:31–32)

In this passage, Jesus seems to allow divorce on the grounds of "unchastity," an exception that finds no place in the Gospel parallels. Luke 16:18 omits the exception.

The "certificate of divorce," prescribed in Deut. 24:1, had the effect of clarifying the woman's status. The husband was unable, once she had that certificate, to make any further claim on her. The certificate was valid in every respect and could not be retracted by a whimsical husband.

The qualifying clause, "except on the ground of unchastity," is regarded by most modern critics as Matthew's addition to the original tradition. "Jesus may have made no exceptions, but the church had to legislate for hard cases. Matthew believed that Jesus had given the church this power."[28]

The Greek word "unchastity" may refer to premarital un-chastity, or it may also include adultery. The intent is unclear. His warning, in v. 32, against remarriage may indicate room for repentance and reconciliation.

This clause arises again in Matt. 19:3–12, where Jesus dis-cusses the issue with the Pharisees. The background to the encounter includes a debate that divided Jewish thought on divorce. The school of Hillel taught that a man could divorce his wife if she found "disfavor" in his eyes. A more stringent position was taken by the Shammai school, which interpreted "disfavor" to mean only the disfavor caused by her adultery. All groups agreed that the male was dominant. Thus, if Christ sided with the latter group, he would offend Herod (who had recently divorced his wife to marry Herodias) and the Hille-lites. If he took lenient ground, he would be at odds with the followers of Shammai, and be accused of laxity in his views.

The commentary in *The Jerusalem Bible* suggests that Jesus seems to allow divorce, with the power to remarry, in cases of adultery. Yet, this comes close to supporting the very conces-sion he is criticizing. Nowhere does he suggest a solution.[29]

It would seem that, in the original setting, Jesus took a harder line, attempting to discourage easy divorce. He did not discuss exceptions. He kept his stress upon the permanence as the ideal of marriage. Matthew's addition of the exception clause would indicate the practical necessity of adapting the absolute rule to the circumstance later facing the church. The church seemed to respond to a concern for persons who were getting the brunt of cold legalistic application of the law, recognizing that there may be grounds upon which divorce is justified. This willingness to respond and to adapt, yet keeping an integrity to the institution of marriage, may be a clue for the church today. To take a "hard line," and to not condone divorce on any grounds, may be insensitive to changing circumstances which merit concern and consideration. Yet, neither can the church indiscriminately approve divorce. The times are changing again for the church and its dealing with divorce.

> It seems that the Presbyterian Church of the past was inclined to preach that divorce was wrong, and that remarriage was adulterous, while today's message is one of hope and reconciliation and love. All of this seems to indicate that the Presbyterian Church is becoming more cognizant of the psychological burdens of divorce and more ready to surround the parties of a broken marriage with love and support. The question to be asked now is: are the practices and policies of local churches matching the official statements of their church?[30]

In an attempt to discover what churches are or are not doing to minister to separated and divorced people, Garner Scott Odell surveyed ninety-three clergy in the Bay area, and seventy-four separated or divorced persons. Results showed that over forty percent of the clergy responding to the questionnaire indicated that they could more effectively minister to single and divorced people if they had more understanding, knowledge, and interaction with single and divorced people.[31]

Britton Wood, writing on the church's ministry to the formerly married (widowed and divorced), supports the need for increased awareness of the needs of these single adults. He notes that the formerly married tend to feel out of place in most churches because adequate programming has not been developed to meet their needs. Although changes are occurring rapidly, many churches are programmed to meet the needs of married family units. He gives a rather biting perception for local church leaders to ponder:

> Church leadership is often uncomfortable with the responsibility of styling a program that meets the needs of single adults. Most churches are inadequately staffed even to meet the needs

of two-adult families. It is not surprising that they are reluctant to jump into a whole new arena of ministry.[32]

THE ADULT WHO IS SINGLE BY DEATH

There are almost twice as many widowed men and women in the United States as there are divorced persons—11.7 million to 5.9 million. A special 1974 U.S. Bureau of the Census report on marital status and living arrangements in our country showed almost three times as many women are widowed (9.8 million) as divorced (3.6 million). There are approximately 2 million divorced men.

Lynn Caine writes of her experience after her husband died leaving her with two young children. She notes how difficult it was to face the sudden singleness in which she was thrown. Even the term "widow" struck her as a harsh and hurtful word. It comes from the Sanskrit root that means "empty."[33]

> Widows have to face up to the fact that they have what sociologist Robert Fulton calls "a spoiled identity." Widows, he explains, "are stigmatized by the death of the ones they loved." It is true. The widow is stigmatized and she has to fight against society's automatic tendency to consider her taboo because her husband is dead. . . . *The progression from wife to widow and back to woman is a hard one.* It is impossible for some widows and they sink into that lonely ghetto of widowhood until they too die.[34]

Since Biblical times, the widow has had a hard time finding a place in society. In the Old Testament, widows were frequently subjected to harsh treatment socially. The Hebraic culture did not seem to incorporate a strong concern for the widow. In every code except the Hebraic, the widow has rights of inheritance, but in Deuteronomic law she is completely ignored. One reason cited for this strange neglect may be attributed to the Hebrew belief that death before old age was a calamity, a judgment for sin which extended to the surviving widow. It was therefore a disgrace to be a widow. (See Ruth 1:20–21; Isa. 54:4.)

On the other hand, several laws did consider the widow's plight within Hebraic society and recognize her existence. The levirate law of Deut. 25:5–10, which provides that, if two Jewish brothers live together and one of them dies leaving no son, the other brother shall marry the widow. The first son of this eventual union would take the name of the brother who died, thus allowing for the continuance of the family name. The widow, however, was without recourse if there were no brothers of her ex-husband or if his family was too poor to support her. Also a childless widow was given considerable security, if she was the daughter of a priest. Leviticus 22:13 provides that she could return to her father's house, where she might wait for a levirate marriage.

Basically, the widow held an inferior position in the community. She evidently had only the protection which public compassion afforded her by acts of charity and justice. Frequently, it was the latter which was experienced. Such treatment brought strong condemnation from the prophets and other writers against injustice. They saw that, in the day of judgment, God would take swift action against those who oppress the widow (Mal. 3:5).

Yet, there was occasional concern expressed for the widow. Those who had to live in poverty and an unprotected position were regarded as under special guardianship by God. "Father of the fatherless and protector of widows is God in his holy habitation" (Ps. 68:5. See also Ps. 146:9; Deut. 10:18; Jer. 49:11). Deuteronomy 26:12 stipulates that the practical needs of the widow were to be looked after as a member of the covenant community: "When you have finished paying all the tithe of your produce in the third year, giving it to the Levite, the sojourner, the fatherless, and the widow, that they may eat within your towns and be filled."

Due regard for the needs of widows was looked upon as a mark of true religion, ensuring a blessing for those who showed it, as well as for the widow. (See Job 29:13; Isa. 1:17; Jer. 22:3.) On the other hand, neglect of and cruelty or injustice toward widows were considered marks of wickedness meriting punishment from God. (See Job 22:9; Ps. 94:6; Isa. 1:23; Mal. 3:5.) The book of Deuteronomy is especially rich in such counsel, insisting that widows be granted full justice (Deut. 24:17; 27:19).

Within the early New Testament community, there was a growing awareness of and concern for those who were widows. The earliest mention of widows in the history of the Christian church is found in Acts 6:1, where the Hellenists (Greek-speaking Jews) were critical of the Hebrews (Jews who spoke Hebrew or Aramaic) because the latter neglected their widows in the daily distribution of alms or food. The tension between the two groups is reflected in Acts, chs. 6 and 7.

There was an evident concern in the early church for widows. In the course of time, these elderly pensioners became an excessive burden on the finances of the church. Paul deals with the matter in I Tim. 5:3–16. He charges relatives and Christian friends to help relieve those widows with whom they are personally connected, so that the church might be more able to relieve those who were "real widows" (i.e., widows in actual poverty and without anyone responsible for their support).

Some scholars interpret the passage as suggesting that there was an official order of widows who had special charitable duties in return for maintenance by the church.[35] In any case, the early church definitely sought to express its care for those who were widows by supportive means.

If widowhood is a single state to be dealt with in society, it is also a special problem to be coped with by the person concerned. Each widow faces distinctive stresses according to the circumstances surrounding the death of her spouse. Widowhood following a long illness brings one set of problems, suicide another. Of course, there are countless other types of death, some more sudden than others, some more socially acceptable than others.

The widow has to cope with not only being alone but also caring for herself in a setting that is now void of spouse. Noting a similarity between both widowed and divorced, Britton Wood observes that "when one's marital status is changed from married to widowed or divorced, a great loss of identity often follows. The self-confidence of the formerly married is often very low due to failure in marriage or rejection in death."[36]

Betty Bryant, a widow, writes of her experience. Drawing insights from several theological sources, she tells how the shock of death comes often without preparation.

> No wife can take it for granted that she will be outlived by her husband, for statistics prove otherwise. She cannot assume that he will live to a ripe old age and die peacefully in his sleep, but neither can she anticipate that he will die young, and tragically. She *can* take it for granted that she will be unprepared for it whenever and however death comes.[37]

The stages of grief outlined by Elisabeth Kübler-Ross have helped us to better understand what many people who are single again go through following the death of a spouse.

One of the most natural and common stages of the grief process is anger. As Lynn Caine explains:

> One researcher who observed 22 young and middle-aged widows discovered that 18 of them experienced "excessive anger" during their first year of widowhood. One woman was angry at her late husband for not telling his dreams about his headaches earlier. Several were angry at the nurses and physicians who had

cared for their husbands. Other became infuriated at friends and relatives. Some were angry at God.[38]

As in divorce, widowhood can bring feelings of rage over being abandoned: "How dare he die on me!" "How dare he leave me to this miserable life!" Both a marital breakup and a death of spouse can call forth strong feelings of anger and hostility. Such anger, unless worked with, can get internalized as a physical ailment of some kind. It can get denied or suppressed until it emerges in more devious and destructive ways. Or, it can be pushed down and emerge in the form of depression. It is important that the person alone be assisted to work with these feelings and channel them in constructive directions.

Betty Bryant found that many of her feelings of anger and guilt took some time to emerge and be seen for what they were. She had been taking a class at the time of her husband's suicide. The class was on problems of drug abuse, alcoholism, crime, and suicide. Six days after her husband's death, the topic for the lecture was suicide.

> My classmates seemed extremely uncomfortable because of my presence. They hesitated to meet my eyes with their own. They avoided speaking. As the professor ticked off the symptoms and advance warnings of potential suicide I compared them to my situation and found they correlated. I began to experience my first feelings of guilt: why had I not tried harder—one more doctor or one more clinic—was there really nothing I could have done? And worse—had I really wanted to prevent it?[39]

Feelings of guilt are common among widows and widowers. They wonder whether or not something more could have been done to prevent the spouse's death. At other times, there come feelings of being glad or relieved the person is no longer around. This is particularly true after a long and trying illness. The guilt often comes from having such thoughts. Such thoughts are hard to admit or express.

> From within and without there are pressures on the widow not to talk. It takes strength to disregard them. Some women have such emotional sturdiness that they immediately set about the work of defining their loss and repeating its circumstances until the cruel edge is blunted enough for them to handle its reality. Other women require months before they can bring themselves to talk about their husbands, about their deaths. And until they can talk they have not really started on the road to recovery.[40]

The road to recovery is difficult. Often it must be treaded upon alone. People stand by the side but they don't know what to say or do. It is a road where one becomes very much aware that he or she is alone. That can often bring feelings of self-pity and isolation.

> Since every death diminishes us a little, we grieve—not so much for the dead as for ourselves. And the widow's grief is the sharpest of all, because she has lost the most. . . . Society's distaste for death is so great that widows tend to become invisible women.[41]

Though they know that their spouse is dead, still there is a part of the mind that resists, that won't accept. Lynn Caine describes her frenzy of activity, her moving, her refusal to listen to friends who said, "Take it easy." She eventually learned this was only a frantic postponement of the time when she would have to face widowhood.

One of the most painful of times often comes when the widow or widower is asked to do something with old friends. There are continued reminders that one is single in a couple society. Betty Bryant relates a time when two couples had taken her to lunch. They had been very close at one time to her and her husband. It was a dreary Monday, rainy and gray. She writes in her journal:

> Today at lunch I felt so lonely and left out; for the first time I understood why widows seek the company of other women rather than mixed groups. The camaraderie of husband and wife is too painful to observe; it is best not to be around. My whole instinct is to withdraw, retreat, pull back.[42]

That tendency to withdraw from pain is natural. But growth comes in learning to face it and work through it. No person can survive in an emotionally healthy way by avoiding every painful human encounter. Persons have to be helped to find the resources to go "through the valley of the shadow of death." The resources offered by support groups, mutual friends, and the church can be valuable at such a time, if they are offered with sensitivity.

The pressure to be paired again comes often upon the widowed person. It can come with subtle side implications. Lynn Caine articulates some of this out of her experience.

> This pressure to remarry, with its implications that I could not manage on my own and that I would not be acceptable unless I did remarry, was the cruelest "consolation" of all—and the most commonly proffered one. "Don't worry, Lynn. You're bound to remarry." I heard it over and over. What right did these eager advice-givers have to tell me what to do? I didn't need this meddling.
>
> More than anything else, however, it brought home to me the fact that married women regard widows as a threat, just as they regard divorcées as a threat.[43]

There are strong forms of dependency within the traditional nuclear family structure. Such dependency, with rigid roles defined for men and women is being challenged by the liberation movement of our ear. As we move toward a society where one's identity is not dependent upon the nuclear family we may initially find a clash or threat between those who hold to the nuclear family for their identity and survival and those who begin to find identity in their own sense of being and worth. Gail Sheehy, writing in *Passages* about the sense of renewal that can come to a person who reassesses his or her life direction, suggests that this can be a constructive time in a person's life.

> It is imperative that a woman find a sense of importance and a means of independent survival before the empty nest leaves her feeling superfluous. Otherwise, she may let her fears dictate the very future she most dreads: becoming helplessly reliant on the continued health and constancy of her husband and the largess of her grown children. Every woman fears becoming the proverbial widow who barges in on the family life of her married children, or who treads on the periphery, saying stoutly, "They have their own lives." Whether she has enough money to float around the world on cruise ships or has to sit feeding pigeons from a park bench, she is still the little old girl waiting to die.[44]

Looking at some of the dilemmas confronting the woman who is alone, Patricia O'Brien writes:

> Widows are, in fact, probably the most physically restricted, most helpless women alone. The rights a woman receives in marriage and most of her duties in this role in our society cease upon the death of the husband, sociologist Helena Z. Lopata has said. In other words, widows suffer total role loss, an overwhelming event. Moreover, widows over the age of sixty-five have been discriminated against financially. Until recently they received much less on the average than men in Social Security payments. In a sense, they have been caught coming and going: encouraged to stay home and raise their children and later penalized for not having worked.[45]

The widowed person has tremendous potential and often the gift of experience. To help a person continue to find and develop potential, as well as to utilize wisdom which has come from experience, is a challenge in a ministry with singles. Often, in the marriage situation which was demanding, the widow may not have learned to tap those resources.

The church could help see that channels are found which enable these gifts to be directed. Guidance for the working through of grief, activities that foster friendships, spiritual support for the release of guilt and the building of hope, are all vital in helping to meet the needs and concerns of persons who are single by death. It could further assist by offering legal and financial help to widows, including insurance guidance and estate planning.

The Adult Who Is Young and Single

No survey of the needs and concerns of single adults would be complete without a focus on the single adult who is young (eighteen to thirty years of age). This age group seems to be one of the most difficult to "reach" from the standpoint of the church's ministry with single adults. In my research I found almost nothing of value available in research data.

According to the 1970 Census, young adults make up the largest component, seventy percent, of the population that is forty years of age or younger. There are more than a million divorced persons under the age of thirty-five who have not remarried. "This segment is so ill-defined that we do not have an adequate terminology with which to discuss it. The phrases 'young adult' and 'post adolescent' have a pejorative tone about them, as though the persons so designated have not quite grown up."[46]

Just where to focus on a ministry with young single adults has been a dilemma for the church. Young singles are not present in many churches. Many pastors respond in frustration with their seeming "fickleness."

An editor of *Christianity Today* suggests that many churches ought to abandon the traditional "college and career" grouping. "Any church that wants to serve single adults ought first to undo that euphonious combination."[47] The article notes that about the only thing both college student and a career person have in common is their initial letter. It goes on to warn against a common danger:

> A singles' program should not become primarily a dating bureau; that offends those who have no interest in marriage and makes open friendship between the sexes strained and difficult. Isolating people into homogeneous groups—whether single or married—may be the easy but not necessarily the best way. Everyone needs contact with persons unlike himself. Married people with children should know couples who have none. And single people need married friends.[48]

Of course, this assumes that young single adults would want to participate in such a capacity. Some might. Many probably would not. There are factors that seem to be uniquely focused within the world of young adults. These are people

> for whom the traditional religions, religious organizations, and religious points of view have not provided resolutions for stresses and tensions or ways to handle the ambiguities of life—indeed, for those who have not found much support from any of the established institutions.[49]

In an attempt to better understand the relationships between the church and young adults with varying degrees of interest in the church, the Youth Relations Unit of The United Presbyterian Church U.S.A. conducted a survey with three selected groups of young adults. The first, Group A, were young adults who were "the regular customers," fully responsible participating members in the church. The second, Group B, were young adults only moderately connected with the church. Group C, the "noncustomers," had no connection at all with the church. Data were gathered through interviews, in groups of from six to eight persons. Eleven interview sessions were conducted. The responses seemed to fall into a pattern as shown in Table 2.

The process of interviewing seemed most valuable in learning about Group A. Less was learned about the second group, and still less about the third.

The young adults in Group A seemed to have worked through a stronger sense of identity formation than did those in Groups B or C. They gave indications of being a part of what Gail Sheehy calls "the identity achieved" group. They have been in crisis and come through it, developing a sustained personal stance with regard to their sense of purpose

TABLE 2

Group A: *Church Group*	Group B: *Middle-of-the-Roaders*	Group C: *Nonchurch group*
Have both a group and personal identity in church	Seeking some kind of community in the church	Feelings range from disinterest to hostility
Found community in the church	Work with developing community in church, do not create artificial community	Hopeless about the church
As active giving/ receiving members		
Seeking implications of this community of life	Have feeling of powerlessness, but have hopes	
Community need is where young adults were, and the church *wants* this need	Want to be accepted. Want to accept?	
Related to *whole* church	Related to young adult groups	
Accepted by *whole* church[50]		

and world view.[51] They express both a group and a personal identity with the church. They can both give and receive of themselves in the church community and in its mission.

The other two groups may well be in "the moratorium group." "They have not yet made commitments or invested themselves in other people, and about their own values they are still vague."[52] While delaying their commitments, many of these persons actively struggle toward finding "the right ones." They are in a crisis that has yet to be resolved and are taking a stop-out.

The third group may be more indicative of the stage of counterdependency described by Dr. David Erb.[53] In a study done among students at Whitworth College, the later adolescent research findings of Erikson, Kohlberg, Chickering, and Nevitt Sanford were applied to students at a residential liberal arts college. The research implications of intellectual and emotional development were explored in relation to religious faith development during the college years. Some tentative conclusions were drawn from the study.

> Number One: There does seem to be a pattern of faith development in the college years and it is our speculation that it continues throughout adult life. The stages seem to have the quality of building upon one another and they are fluid, depending upon the life situation of the person.
>
> The second finding: Faith development stages are heavily influenced by the emotional and intellectual development of the person and the stages are not correlated with chronological age after early adolescence.[54]

A brief description of the stages of development is helpful toward understanding the spectrum existing among single young adults. It somewhat correlates with those interviewed on the survey conducted by the Presbyterians.

Briefly, the first stage, dependence, is characterized by

the reliance upon external authority to define one's values, self-worth, and life direction. The "authority" might be parents, peers, or the church. This faith development stage is characterized by a deep reliance upon an ultimate authority to take care of oneself, solve life problems, and give direction to every view of life. There is a strong emphasis upon feelings. It is easy for a young adult who is uncertain about being neither a child nor an adult to seek out a faith experience that will give security and certainty. They are critical of worship experiences that do not allow them to express their feelings.

The second stage, counterdependency, is characterized by doubts, questions, anxiety, and loneliness. It is a time of pushing away from those persons, institutions, and beliefs around which one found himself or herself previously dependent. These acts may come out as extreme criticism of parents, the church, God, or a moral system, in order to move toward the identifying with a model that is one's "own." Where one was previously dependently involved in a faith community that encouraged emotional expression, now there is rejection and disdain of such institutions. Yet, this stage is frequently another form of dependency. One rejects one system in order to move toward another. Feelings toward God become less focused. The person wonders if a relationship with God has been lost. There is much anxiety and doubt about previously adhered to theological positions. Value questions become internal conflicts. The person looks back at the faith commitment which was recently abandoned and harshly judges those persons who still hold to that faith. People who express their faith in a dependent form are seen as weak, naive, and blind by persons in the counterdependent stage.

Most college students seem to fall in these first two stages. They are in that process which Gail Sheehy describes as "seeking an idea to believe in":

> We seek an idea to believe in, heroes and heroines to copy,
> and we begin to rule out what we don't want to do with our
> lives.
>
> Most young people search avidly for a cause greater than
> themselves in the service of which it will make sense to be an
> adult.[55]

It is that search which, in late teen years, seems to keep a young
person in a dependency relationship to the peer group. One
way students do this is by rebelling and doing the opposite of
what the authority figures would wish them to do. Another
familiar counterdependent behavior is to act as if one is totally
independent. "I'm doing my own thing and I don't need
anyone" is the response of a person in this stage.

That dependency begins to erode as one moves toward the
third stage, self-dependence or independence. Though it is a
strong concern of many young people, Erb suggests that independence is rarely seen among college students.[56]

Persons in this stage begin to find a high degree of trust in
their values, feelings, and ideas. They are comfortable with
themselves and have a sense of internal self-worth. They feel
at ease with both emotional dependence and independence;
thus, they possess the capability of being able to satisfy their
own needs as independent persons but also may enjoy the
dependency associated with intimacy.

It is my observation, from discussions with many single
young adults, that this is the stage they frequently move in and
out of. It is the crucial process stage involved in defining a
satisfactory sense of singleness. Many young singles struggle
with developing emotional independence, yet maintaining
some degree of intimacy. It is part of the struggle to integrate
values and behavior.

During this third stage, feelings are viewed as a source of
information about one's response to Ultimate Authority and
to the faith community, rather than as a definition of God.

These feelings are differentiated and attached to present events in one's life. Feelings of anger toward God can arise, then subside. Theology is not grasped as a tight system of answers but is more fluid, flexible, open to growth.

The final stage is described as interdependence. This stage is a "process of two or more self-dependent persons relating to each other. These relationships place a high value on the celebration of differences and allow each person to remain self-dependent, yet with enough dependency to achieve maximum intimacy."[57]

Important intellectual and faith commitments can be made, and these commitments are continually being examined. One begins to integrate or synthesize an understanding of God and self with a larger world view.

As we reflect back on the interviews conducted with young adults by the Presbyterians, it would seem that they are descriptive of the spread among young adults. Those in Group C (Table 2) seem indicative of persons in the later dependent or counterdependent stages. They seem to be pushing against authority. The church represents one of those authority figures in society. The church is associated with an "old and outmoded style" which they are rejecting. Yet they struggle for something to believe in. Because they have rejected much of their rootage, and don't see too much in the future, a lot seems hopeless and directionless for many such young adults.

Helpful in understanding this sense of frustration are insights which Scott Hope presents in a paper entitled "And So On (A Beginning to Work On)." Hope and his ordained Presbyterian minister wife, Glenda, were instrumental in the development of a single and young adult house church ministry in San Francisco, California.

The paper lists thirteen polarities of needs with which young adults of our era are confronted. In brief, these polarities are:

1. *Search for Life's Meaning vs. the Here and Now.* Many young adults express that they seem not to have a reason for being, and an idea to believe in. The referent standpoint is difficult when set beside the current psychology emphasis on the "here and now." Further, "meaning" increasingly becomes the property of external forces and movements rather than the result of inner inquiry.

Many young adults opt for "experience," "sensation," and "free sample" approaches to life. One "goes somewhere" to find meaning.

2. *Wholeness vs. Fragmentation.* Nearly every institution and segment of our society begs us to expose a part of ourselves to its warm and mothering bosom. While trying to "get oneself together," it is easy to become fragmented between the parts of one's culture which call for allegiance.

3. *Mind vs. Body vs. Emotion vs. Spirit.* During recent years we have exalted body and emotion nearly to the exclusion of mind and spirit. We see the exodus from religious institutions, an apathy toward the classics, whether of music, literature, or art. Churches that don't respond to the spiritual questionings they have get left for those which seem to dish out the latest concern.

4. *Future as Hope vs. Hope as Oppression.* Those who feel most urgently the despairs in their contemporary experiences look to the future with the hope that "things must get better." The straight line into tomorrow is drawn with desperate optimism.[58] Over against that hope, however, stand those who find little in current trends to justify such hope and optimism. Nuclear holocausts, diminished food supplies, pollution, ecological disasters, overpopulation, and so on make the future threatening and seem to make hope an illusion. This fear moves many young adults to choose the here and now, the immediate source of gratification.

5. *Mobility vs. Rootedness, the Temporary vs. the Permanent,*

the Disconnected vs. the Connected. Young adults, like so much of our culture, increasingly build their lives around portable entities (and port these entities in campers and vans), around instant relationships, around shifting communes. Values that depend on continuity, permanence, and roots do not have much chance in such worlds.

With the downplay on the importance of history, tradition, and heritage there is a loss of connectedness, a break with a tradition. However, recent moves in our culture toward simpler life-styles, antique furnishings, and the influence of *Roots* may be an evidence of a yearning to recapture a sense of rootedness, permanence, and connection.

6. *Work as Fulfillment vs. Work as Survival.* As the work ethic diminishes in importance, and as more and more persons express discontent with their work lives, there is a tendency away from work as the center of one's existence.

7. *Privacy vs. Loneliness.* No nation in history has so successfully realized the idea of privacy as has this nation. At the same time, no nation has so publicly admitted to loneliness as its most persistent personal pain. This admission is nowhere so loud and articulate as it is among young adults. They are evidence of the lonely people, "the lonely crowd," to use David Riesman's term.

For many young adults, privacy is equated with personhood. Many understand the ability to be private, to be a bridge between the home they are born into and the state of being an adult. This need for satisfaction is symbolized best by the apartment. It may be the expression of breaking from dependency and moving toward independence.

8. *Individualism vs. Community, Independence vs. Dependence.* In significant ways, the sense of community is being taken over by the various entities that have much to gain by perpetuating the concepts of individualism, autonomy, and independence.

Pseudo-communities dot the landscape. Workshops, neighborhood organizations, "swinging singles" residences, all represent what might be called attempts to construct instant and artificial communities. The "rugged individual" does not have to seek or to make a community, it is given to him. The question of whether one lives alone or with others arises at one time or another for nearly all young adults.

This combination seems to run parallel with the movement from Erb's second to third stage.

9. *Technology vs. "Magic."* Basically, this axis speaks to the question: How are we going to invent, realize, secure a future which we find acceptable? Nearly all young adults agree that the world is in a mess. Many of them no longer read the daily newspaper nor watch the news on television. There is a desire for instant remedies.

The ways and contradictions between and among the various "ways of making it better" pose incredible and difficult choices for many young adults. Neither the shareholders in General Electric nor those who promote a belief in God would admit that they are in competition with each other. The tension between "something will happen" and "we must make something happen" is a major source of tension for young adults. There is confusion among them in connection with how to alter the courses of current history.

10. *Immediate Gratification vs. Postponed Gratification.* Young adults face a genuine economic dilemma. Does one purchase what one wants now or does one set aside money for a later time? In a time of inflation, this question becomes especially difficult, especially with a tax structure that seems tilted against singles.

Increasingly, young adults seem to be making a commitment to momentary pleasures and desires at the cost of long-range commitments. Renting and leasing have become honorable. A survey of a sampling of young adults in San Francisco indicated that fewer than a third of those questioned even had a savings account.

> What makes single persons most attractive to business is the fact that they don't hesitate to spend. Much of their income goes for luxury goods—merchandise and services that most married couples daydream about but seldom can afford while raising a family.[59]

This move toward immediate gratification also manifests itself in the decline in participation in religious communities which ask for long-term involvements.

11. *Nuclear Family vs. Extended Family.* As has been previously noted, many young adults seriously challenge the nuclear family as the basic cultural unit. Exiting from the family unit is increasingly an act of rebellion (or counterdependency) rather than a rite of passage. Many young adults struggle to find new families, new ways of defining families. Many explore sequential and shifting families and tentative, short-term relationships. Communal relationships have become a form of "family" sought out by many young adults. For those who choose not to move toward the commune style, finding extended family relationships through a church or other established institution has become an alternative.

12. *The Marriage Ritual vs. the Mating Ritual.* With marriage undergoing considerable challenge as the ultimate context for intimate relationships many young adults find themselves moving away from the point of view that one is not an adult until one has married.

Abortion, ready access to birth control, the easing of economic injunctions against living together, the power of the feminist movement urging movement away from traditional roles, and the sexual revolution all can be cited as examples that encourage the young adult to hurry into permanent relationships. With the highest divorce rate coming from teen-age marriages, many young adults have become suspicious of making a marriage commitment. In addition, the varieties of sexual interactions (homosexual, bisexual, heterosexual) and the decreasing emphasis upon virginity seem to contribute to make marriages less appealing and unifying as a cultural force.

13. *Ritual vs. Novelty*

> Americans do not like to do anything more than once. Increasingly, "experience" is being substituted for ritual. Because we do not like to do something more than once, we become easily bored. Because we are easily bored, we are easily dissuaded from probing the depths of anything.[60]

Thus, a Woodstock or an Altamont, or any number of one-time events, take on the aura of a ritual, complete with high priests. Those who participate ritualize the memory of the event, forming a congregation on the basis "Were you there when . . . ?"

Hope suggests that the problems connected with such growth and being needs serve to contribute deeply to the anxieties, angers, and anomalies of young adults. Young adults are a part of this dynamic process. With the process prolonged up into the mid-twenties, young adults develop a culture of their own. The sorting out of needs is not easy. "Most of us during this period of exploration are vague, if not void of ideas about what we want to do. We generally begin by defining what we don't want to do."[61]

Somewhere, however, the process of affirmation and self-actualization needs to happen, as one moves toward a sense of independence and wholeness. The world of the single young adult is indeed complex.

The church faces a large challenge in relating to and including young singles in its ministry. A sensitivity to the polarities and complexities of decisions facing today's young adults would help the church to have more credibility among them. Many single adults who are young look to the church for that kind of sensitivity. They want help in working through the answers. Moralistic judgments that do not seem sensitive simply reinforce a notion that the church does not care or understand.

Lauri Warder, writing in *The Christian Ministry*, states that "young adults are not looking for the church to structure their social life, but rather that they not be excluded from those activities in which they would like to participate."[62] She adds this challenge:

> All of us, even those who aren't single, would like someone to help us learn the meaning of hope; help us adjust to our existence, share our problems and our joys.
>
> The church can help us face up to who we are and where we are, can keep us from alienating ourselves from the world around us and hiding behind our singleness.
>
> Maybe all we're asking is that that the church reach out to us as it does to others.[63]

THE ADULT WHO IS SINGLE AND A PARENT

Emerging as an important factor in American life is a rapidly growing number of single parents—the divorced, the widowed, the unwed mothers and bachelor fathers.

The term "single parent" indicates that only one parent lives with the child or children while the other parent is not a participating part of the family living unit. Usually these family units are created by divorce or death. Increasing numbers are due to desertion, separation because of marital conflict, long-term separation due to occupation, and separation by institutionalization such as confinement to correctional institutions or hospitalization for mental or physical illness. Also included are single persons who adopt a child, and unwed mothers.

Since 1965, the number of single-parent families has increased 31.4 percent, almost triple the growth reported for two-parent families. Single-parent families account for 14.9 percent of the nation's 54 million families, or about 8.1 million. That includes about 8.6 million children under eighteen years of age.

Table 3 figures would indicate that the fastest growth in one-parent families has come among divorced or separated males and unwed mothers. There are, according to the 1970 Census statistic, 5,260,000 single mothers. A later Census Bureau figure puts that number up to 7.2 million.[65] That means that about one out of every seven families in America is headed by a woman.

TABLE 3

FIGURES ON ONE-PARENT FAMILIES[64]

Families Headed by Fathers Alone

	1965	*1972*	*Change*
Widowers	443,000	480,000	Up 8%
Divorced,			
Separated Males	208,000	365,000	Up 71%
Single Males	426,000	410,000	Down 4%

Families Headed by Mothers Alone

Widows	2,301,000	2,370,000	Up 3%
Divorced,			
Separated Females	1,731,000	2,743,000	Up 58%
Single Females	397,000	713,000	Up 80%

Rising illegitimacy rates among teenagers and a greater tendency for women to establish their own households rather than live with relatives have played a role in this increase. But by far, the major cause of the growing number of female-headed households has been the skyrocketing divorce rate, now dissolving about one in three American families.[66]

The traditional view has been that a divorced mother is more suitable for child-rearing than a divorced father. When Ray and his wife decided to get a divorce, their teen-age daughter requested to live with him. That decision was difficult to accept, particularly for those who felt that "a daughter should live with her mother." Such sex-role stereotypes are being challenged more and more.

However, the fact still holds that when a divorce or separation occurs, ninety percent of the time mothers get custody of the children.

In most states, laws are changing to allow single persons to adopt children or to become foster parents, particularly to children with a handicap or mixed racial ancestry.

Even one parent who really loves a child is much better than institutional care. There is also a growing trend for single women to intentionally bear a child. Some Christians are beginning to wonder if artificial insemination might be permissible for such single women who desperately want a child of their own but yet don't want to commit fornication.[67]

Single parenting is an increasing reality in our society, bringing with it a whole set of new ethical questions.

Single parents not only have to confront the particular needs of being single in a pairing society, but do so with the added responsibility of raising children. For many single parents, life is bitter and difficult as they encounter an avalanche of financial, social, and psychological problems.

For a woman who has been married and is now single, single

parenthood may be part of a whole new journey in a strange land. Coping with financial responsibilities, finding or keeping a full-time job, maintaining enough emotional space from the children, and handling decisions about sexual relationships can seem awesome. Susan Griffin, in her article "Confessions of a Single Mother," writes: "To stay off welfare, most women must find work. But before she can accept work, a mother must find decent day care, and her search is often fruitless."[68]

Martha, a widow with two teen-age children, reflected on her experience of suddenly being thrown into single parenthood: "The man still has his job, but there is no continuity in the work world, particularly for the widowed mother who worked part time before. Once you're a widow, you don't have the same support system as before. You're now in a category by yourself. As a mother and a widow, there isn't much independent life. People tried to comfort me . . . they were frightened and didn't know what to say. There was not a lot of sustaining comfort for the children either. Oh, of course, people were kind . . . but they were also distant. . . . If only a man would have called to take them to a football game!"

For the parent with custody rights it's too much children too much of the time. "Single parents often become tired of parenting. They are exhausted from the twenty-four-hour-a-day parent pressure with no help from the ex-spouse."[69] For the parent without custody rights it's too little children too much of the time. One suffers overload and one suffers loneliness. And the hurt is equal on the emotional level.

Many single fathers who are noncustodial say that they suffer most from the emotional sparsity of being a Saturday or weekend parent, of feeling left out and isolated from children they love and want to be with.

Single-parent mothers don't have the same problem as their ex-mates, but they will tell you, they have just about everything else. Usually their feelings are mixed. They are frequently angry at having to be both mother and father and bearing full responsibility for the children at all times, usually without enough money, which makes it an even greater chore.[70]

Many single parents often feel as though they are prisoners in their own home. Robert Pinder reflects on some of the needs of single parents:

Loneliness is probably the most outstanding characteristic of single parents, regardless of the cause of their status. Emotionally, many single parents consistently miss companionship, and put this above all other needs. Specifically, they miss a partnership in the many perplexities of child-rearing, problems which could be dealt with more securely through joint responsibility. . . . Instead of the "normal" dyadic relationship of two parents, there is instead a parent-child dyad or pair.[71]

Parents, as well as children, have needs for security, love, acceptance, and fulfillment. Often those needs go unmet as the single parent is caught up in the demands of parenting and meeting financial needs. Pinder indicates:

The single parent has limited social ties, and will probably have less opportunity for communication and sharing with other adults. The love of the parent for the child and the child for the parent is very gratifying to the single parent but is not as supportive as adult-to-adult relationships. The single parent is generally deprived of adult relationships to meet his/her own needs.[72]

Single parents may need help in sorting out their personal needs. In a lopsided dependent relationship, one person requires the support and enforcement of the other for an adequate sense of identity. This often results in the need of one to manipulate the other so as not to lose him and to force him to fulfill the dependent one's needs and wants. When this kind of neurotic dependency gets expressed in a single parent and child relationship professional assistance may be needed. As Carole Klein warns:

> Rigidly neurotic needs that must be satisfied allow no real growth. A person who needs love and constant proof of love will suffocate a child, and even when done in the name of love, this behavior will cut off a child's chances for a healthy life of his own.[73]

Persons who have not sorted out their dependency needs can be vulnerable to exploitive relationships. The demands of single parenthood, and especially the lack of a parent of the opposite sex often push a person who has been divorced or widowed into a quick second marriage.

Yet, many single parents who were previously married see the time of aloneness as a time to sort themselves out, to understand their strengths and weaknesses, to assess their interaction with others. Many who can work out child-care arrangements seek out support groups. They are willing to use their singleness as a means of growth toward interdependence. Mel Krantzler observes that "parents who take care of themselves will be best able to take care of their children."[74]

It is a challenge to the church to provide such people good opportunities for emotional, social, and spiritual growth. Anyone who would seek to help single parents in their growth process would do well to understand the nature of some stages frequently experienced by single adults who are either divorced, widowed, or deserted. A summary of these stages, as given in a lecture by James Ewing, helps highlight their basic characteristics.

Stage One: *Shock and Anxiety.* Initially the person may experience panic and uncontrolled anxiety, denial of loss, crying and intense prayer, or such symptoms as disturbed sleep, headaches, poor eating habits, nervousness, lack of concentration. This period varies in length among individuals depending upon their past history of recovery from intense stress and their ability at self-control.

Stage Two: *Depression and Loneliness.* Here the person enters his or her valley of despair, characterized by a loss of self-esteem and well-being, a growing hostility toward the former spouse, a disbelief in being able to adjust, a growing envy of happy families, a withdrawl from traditional social contacts and even close friends, a feeling of hopelessness. God may be the only constant reality.

Stage Three: *Time of Readjustment.* As psychologists note, our bodily system seeks to maintain a balance between our needs for acceptance and love and the pressures of rejection and failure. One can draw upon inner strength and God's power. With the added support of friends and one's "community," the person begins the road to recovery. Often a realignment of roles is realized and accepted during this time. Parenthood, work, social relationships all press to be defined in terms of the new reality. Many single parents find they go through a value change in which old values they felt were important become less important and new values take on increased meaning. The conflict over the possibility of remarriage is usually resolved when dating starts again. The dilemma for Christians over postmarital sexual involvement rarely subsides.

Stage Four: *Recovery.* Self-esteem returns, especially when old and new friends find them worthy and lovable again. There is a recovery of hope and the reestablishment of some new and meaningful relationships.[75]

Persons going through these stages may be helped by realizing where they are in the adjustment process, becoming aware of their own resources, and developing the skills needed to meet the tasks at hand. Often the single parent needs help in learning to trust his or her own feelings as well as to trust others.

Unfortunately there are many pastors, church leaders, and

others who consistently neglect divorced (and widowed) persons and their families either because they lack a sympathetic, open understanding of the needs of these persons, or because they are not able to translate their empathy for these persons into positive actions of acceptance and ministry.

> Churches that are successful in reaching and ministering to single parents strive to build this atmosphere of acceptance and to demonstrate love in action. Acceptance and love are the primary ingredients. When single parents feel censored or rejected or are treated as second-class citizens, they drop out or make some excuse to avoid intimate fellowship.[76]

If the church can help the single parent to care for his or her own personhood, as well as encourage him or her to be involved in a single adult ministry with other understanding friends, a great service can be provided to parent and child(ren). Being in touch with other single parents can prove helpful. Those who are learning to cope successfully with single parenthood can be of help to the one who is beginning to face the realities of a new situation. The church can also help in practical ways such as being aware of community resources and agencies that can provide special kinds of services for single parents, provide counseling services in economic concerns, and child care for children.

With more openness and understanding from the church, single parents can be helped toward growth and find that "parenting can become bearable and begin to be fun."[77]

5

AS A SINGLE, COULD I FIND HELP FROM THE BIBLE?

(RETHINKING BIBLICAL AND THEOLOGICAL STARTING POINTS)

SARAH SAT in the pew, alone. The organ prelude for the worship service gave her time to gather some thoughts. It had been a hard week for her. The decision not to marry Bill had not come easily. He was wanting to get married, but she didn't feel she was ready for that decision. In spite of pressure from her family and friends, Sarah decided to wait. She wasn't sure marriage was the answer for her at this stage in her life.

Bill had not taken the news lightly. Breaking off the engagement, he left town "to find somewhere else to settle down." Sarah felt alone and confused that Sunday morning.

The service began. Sarah felt her throat tighten as she noticed the young couple in front of her, holding hands. She glanced down at her bulletin. The sermon that day would be on "Marriage, God's Key to Human Wholeness." Sarah picked up her purse and quietly slipped out of the sanctuary.

Sarah's pastor may not have been aware of her painful situation that Sunday morning. Nor can he be faulted for preaching on marriage. Possibly his theology on the meaning of human wholeness could be challenged.

Maybe Sarah will be back in worship, at a less vulnerable time. Maybe not.

In an age of change and dehumanization, many other single adults, like Sarah, struggle for a sense of identity, affirmation, and direction. They struggle to find a faith that is both relevant to their needs and challenging to their values.

The church also struggles to find a way to relate more adequately to single adults.

Many church people admit that they frankly "do not know much about singles, except there aren't many around the church!"

There is available an increasing number of articles, books, and other material on single adults, in both the secular and the religious fields, particularly in the past couple of years. The conservative branch of the church seems to. be producing the largest quantity of material on singles, some of which cater to a more literal Biblical interpretation and a more traditional life-style.

In its report to the Church Council of Greater Seattle, the task force on single adults included suggestions for possible future action by the church. In the area of theology, the report suggests:

1. There is definitely a need for rethinking the biblical-theological meaning of "singleness" in the light of today's society. Letting the scriptures speak to the realities of the present may help yield a more inclusive theology. We need to recognize that we are dealing with a human condition for which the scriptural message may not be obvious.

2. A theology of singleness should not be built as over against a theology of marriedness. Current conventions of church and society seem to treat singleness as a transition stage in adulthood. Singleness by choice is frequently not recognized. There is a need for a biblical theology which affirms singleness as a valid life-style for some people.

3. Biblical research needs to be done which can help such a theology emerge. Models of singleness (beyond Jesus and Paul?), the meaning of human wholeness (apart from marriage as a prerequisite), vocation as a calling to every person,

and an affirmation of human sexuality, are particular areas ripe for study.

4. The biblical understanding of divorce and remarriage needs to be rethought in the light of the complexities of many marriage breakdowns today. The Church has often excluded itself from offering the gift of a caring, Christian community from those who most need it. Sensitive ways of including the recognition of marriage termination within worship need to be explored and developed.[1]

One great area of void in the church is a theological perspective on the meaning of singleness. Very little has been written by the church, either ancient or modern, on this subject.

The subject needs to be addressed, since we know that anytime one launches into a new territory the going is apt to be treacherous. Yet, if the church is going to develop an appropriate means of ministry with single adults, it must rethink some of the Biblical, theological, and cultural premises from which it has commonly operated. At the same time, it must trust the Holy Spirit to lead in some possible new directions, "letting the scriptures speak to the realities of the present."

CELIBACY, AN ALTERNATIVE TO MARRIAGE

Marriage and the family are firmly embedded in the matrix of our Biblical and theological heritage. The institution of marriage in the Bible reflects a long history of sociological and cultural development. Many stages and patterns preceded our present style of marriage and family.

In Judeo-Christian tradition, marriage has been viewed as a covenant, and agreement. As an institution within the Jewish community, marriage provided a regulation of sexual behavior, especially for women. As interpreted from Gen. 2:18–25, it provided companionship between a husband and wife. It was also an institution primary in the furtherance of the religious, social, economic, and social life of the people. Built within the religious system was a protection for marriage. It was expected that everyone who could would marry. Single adults were a minority in Old Testament culture.

When we look at the New Testament we see some carry-overs from Old Testament thinking, as well as the emergence of some totally new attitudes. There is evidence of an early dethronement of marriage from its all-important place within Jewish society. This was partly due to a shift away from the agrarian and holistic life to a more cosmopolitan style.

Several of the key New Testament characters were unmarried. Jesus and Paul, as well as John the Baptist before them, do not appear to have been married.

Jesus was born into an extended family. He chose a single adult life-style in community with what sociologists today would call "chosen kin." His closest friends were Peter, James, and John. He seemed most at home in the town of Bethany, with Mary, Martha, and Lazarus.

> He was motivated in his relationships by love, not by loneliness. He knew how to be alone. He did not seek relationships to escape from coming to terms with himself.[2]

Jesus seemed to be fully at home with his own sexuality, totally aware of it and in control. Thus, he could enjoy the loving touch of Mary of Bethany as she washed his weary feet, massaged them with a fragrant ointment, and then tenderly dried them with her flowing hair (John 12:1–3).

As a single man, Jesus did not seem threatened by the possibility of being misinterpreted. He was not hesitant to hold John to his breast as they reclined with the other apostles at the Last Supper (John 13:23–25). Nor was he afraid that his gestures might be misinterpreted as seductive. He could befriend a woman who already had five husbands and was now living with a lover. He could call the attention of his followers to the sacrificial gift of a poor widow, as they observed her stewardship at the Temple treasury. (See John 4:16f. and Mark 12:42.)

Jesus chose the life of a celibate for the duration of his brief ministry. While he was committed to this life-style, he did not force it upon his followers.

In the encounter that follows Jesus' response to the question of divorce in Matt., ch. 19, the matter of not marrying (celibacy) is brought into discussion. The disciples had responded to Jesus' statement on divorce by suggesting that maybe it would be "not expedient to marry" (Matt. 19:10), or as Today's English Version translates, "it is better not to marry," implying that if a person can never escape from an unhappy marriage, maybe it would be "expedient" for the person not to marry at all! Such a recurring attitude can be seen among many single adults today.

Jesus, in his response (Matt. 19:12), suggests three basic reasons for remaining single:

1. *The Circumstance of Birth.* Some persons are born physically incapable of sexual intercourse. Congenital birth defects may discourage a marriage. "This reference to birth might be extended to physiological issues which the ancients would not know about."[3]

2. *The Circumstance of Incapacitation or Mutilation.* The original reference may have been to castration. This might also include impotency from illness, or surgical accident. The effects of economic depression, malnutrition, ill treatment might also apply.

3. *The Circumstance of Religious Commitment.* This latter reason seems highlighted by Jesus. Apart from the eunuch position of the passage, it can also include those who chose singleness for their service to God. John the Baptist, Mary and Martha, and their brother Lazarus, all appear to fall under this circumstance, as do Jesus and Paul.

Jesus warned, "Not all men can receive this precept, but only those to whom it is given" (Matt. 19:11). This may have been said to discourage any "forced interpretations of the teaching. It is an appeal to spiritual intelligence, as if Jesus had said, 'Be careful not to misconceive the meaning.' "[4]

The apostle Paul goes so far as to call compulsory celibacy a heresy. (See I Tim. 4:1–3.) When he advises against marriage (I Cor. 7:26) it is clearly because of impending hard times facing the church.

Commenting on Paul's advice in I Cor., ch. 7, Mark Lee writes:

> Apparently the Apostle Paul, under the conviction that Jesus would soon redeem the physical world by his second coming, preferred celibacy for himself and others. He acknowledged that marriage is a normal estate and that, single or married, one required a gift, perhaps a natural endowment, for his choice (I Cor. 7:7).[5]

Paul, who had been trained to be a rabbi, was unmarried and preferred other Christians to be as he was, in view of: (1) the impending messianic woes (vs. 27–31) and (2) the inevitable distractions in loyalty between spouse and service to the kingdom (vs. 32–35).[6] Yet, Paul is humble enough to admit that, in giving his advice, he has "no command from the Lord, but I give my opinion as one who by the Lord's mercy is trustworthy" (v. 25).

One tension that existed within the Corinthian religious community at the time probably had an effect upon Paul's advice. The Jewish emphasis upon marriage as a duty came from one direction within the church. Yet, among the Gentile community the tendency toward celibacy was so strong that it was necessary to counteract it by legal enactment. The Greco-Roman world was at such a low state of decay that they were having trouble getting people to marry. This view shocked Christian leaders who came from the Jewish tradition. They appeal to Paul for an answer. The questions put to Paul seemed to be whether or not the unmarried should marry, and should the married Christian continue to live with an unbelieving spouse. In I Cor. 7:17, Paul responds by suggesting that the person should ascertain what is best for him or her. He reasons that unmarried men would be more efficient in their service to Christ if they remain as such (vs. 32–33).

From both instances cited relating to Jesus and Paul, it would seem that, taken literally, they encouraged the single life, particularly as a faith commitment. While both figures were themselves committed to a single life-style, they did not force their style upon other believers. They did call people to a deeper commitment in the Lord. For Paul, the urging was toward singleness, as the most sufficient means of living out that commitment. Both leaders seemed to break with their previous traditions by affirming celibacy as an alternative to marriage, and affirming the single condition as a means of serving the Lord.

As we look beyond the New Testament period, a quick glance would indicate that the church initially continued to support a place for singles within its life, particularly for the celibate life.

> The early tendency toward the single state was continued in some segments of the later church. The silence about marriage in the Gospel of John and Johannine epistles may indicate uncertainty in that circle about marriage. . . .
>
> Only Gnostic Christianity seems to have stressed celibacy, though the evidence for this is largely of a post-New Testament date.[7]

One church historian, writing about the spread of Christianity in its first hundred years, notes:

With the married state, the single also, as an exception to the rule, is consecrated by the Gospel to the service of the kingdom of God; as we see in a Paul, a Barnabas, and a John, and in the history of missions and of ascetic piety.

The enthusiasm for celibacy, which spread so soon throughout the ancient church, must be regarded as one-sided, though natural and, upon the whole, beneficial against the rotten conditions and misery of family life among the heathen.[8]

Many Christians beyond the New Testament shared Paul's viewpoint about singleness.

Jerome extolled the joys and virtues of the celibate life for virgins and those whose spouses had died. . . . The monastic life provided opportunities for solitary prayer and devotion, a community in which to find mutual support and avenues of service to others. Church history is studded with stories of single people whose service to God was nourished by communal religious life and by the deepest of friendships.[9]

One of the most unfortunate consequences of the fifteenth-century Protestant Reformation was its disavowal of monastic life and the dissolution of religious communities in most Protestant churches. Focusing only upon the abuses of the monastic system and not its virtues, Protestantism abolished it rather than making an attempt to reform it.

Such an overview would seem to affirm the value of singleness, especially the celibate life. Moving outward from a New Testament affirmation of the celibate life, the church has, at least up through the Protestant Reformation, found a valid avenue to affirm an alternative to marriage. While most of that affirmation has focused around the celibate, at least the church has demonstrated an ability to adapt to changing situations and needs. The statements of Jesus, Paul, and the New Testament community were made in a historical context. They pressed for a change in attitude, extending the focus of the religious community toward a more inclusive attitude of at least part of the singles community.

For the Protestant community, at least in the Western world, some of that inclusiveness slowed down following the Protestant Reformation. The pendulum swung away from the elevation of celibacy, toward a stress upon marriage and family. Seen as a vehicle for spreading the faith, the family became a dominant unit, as it was in Old Testament times. What was unfortunate in that change, however, has been the insensitivity demonstrated by the Christian church to the needs of adults who are single.

Today the need is present for the church to look at its Biblical and theological roots. What may have been a traditional concern for the family may have, since Biblical times, put singleness out of focus. The time has come for the church to look once again at Scripture and seek the wisdom of God's Spirit in developing a theological affirmation of singleness which does not deny or downplay the importance of marriage and family life, but which exists "alongside of" such an emphasis.

Single adulthood is a fact of our time. The church, in recognizing that fact, needs to seek new Biblical and theological insight into the meaning of singleness. As Gary Collins suggests: "The same God who created marriage never implied that the unmarried should be forced to resign themselves to a lusterless second-best kind of existence."[10] It is toward the development of some new possible directions in theological affirmation that we now move, trusting the validity of the past and the challenge of the future.

REALIZING A BIBLICAL AFFIRMATION OF SINGLENESS

The traditional starting points for a more inclusive theology have usually been interpreted from a marriage-oriented culture.

There are culturally biased messages coming out of Scripture. They are also mixed.

Letting the Scriptures speak to us in a new way for a new age is not an easy task for the church and its theology. But as one author suggests: "The church can only recover its own original gospel of the New Creation of the resurrection body by dying to a culture and social change with which it has most deeply identified itself."[11]

If we are to hear God's word, we cannot assume that we know automatically what the word of Scripture will say on any given issue. The Spirit may speak one "word" to a given age, yet another word to the next age.

> The real task of biblical scholarship is no different than that which all Christians undertake when they read the Bible: to hear and understand the Bible as God's own word. The question, however, is whether the Bible is really understood as God's own word when it is regarded simply as a book of rules for moral conduct. [12]

As Professor Darrell Doughty emphasizes, "the New Testament makes the question of law and Gospel the central issue for the Christian faith."[13] He goes on to note that the human sciences can "teach us the relativity of our own cultural assumptions, and thereby resist any easy identification of our own prejudices with the will of God."[14]

The church may be in a situation again in history where it needs to listen carefully to the prodding of God's Spirit. We cannot assume that we know the will of God regarding marriage and family. God may well be pressing the church to develop a theology that allows singleness the same sort of acceptance as marriage and family. The church is not being called to abandon its previous theology but rather to open it up more so that those who are not married can realize that they have a valid place within God's good creation.

While a theology of singleness does not readily emerge, there may be some starting points from which such an affirmation can grow.

Mennonite theologian John H. Yoder notes that "modern western society almost universally presupposes the normativeness of married life as the only proper way to be an adult human being." In contrast, Yoder sees singleness as normative. He suggests:

> It needs to be taught as normative Christian truth that *singleness is the first normal state of every Christian.* Marriage is not wrong, and existing marriages are to be nurtured. Yet there exists no Christian imperative to become married as soon as one can, or to prefer marriage over singleness as a more whole or wholesome situation.
>
> Singleness is better for those who find their fulfillment in it, and singleness is the first duty of every single person until the reasons for marriage are clear.[15]

The fact of singleness being a common state for each person either before or after marriage may at least force us to acknowledge that all of us must be single sometime in our lives. Not all persons are single, but all will live for a time as singles. And, as Mark Lee emphasizes: "Certainly the Christian life and conduct which ought to characterize the believer is not qualitatively different for singles and marrieds."[16] It is such an affirmation of singleness that leads us to explore some of the Biblical concepts from which a theology of singleness might emerge.

Wholeness in Christ

Jesus never said, "In order to follow me you must first go get married." He called people to follow him as the clue to a vital faith in a creating, redeeming God. He set no criteria for

discipleship except a response to God's love. He called people
to respond to God's grace, to repent and receive forgiveness,
and to walk the journey of life by faith. He called people to
wholeness, to health.

Two New Testament words refer to a concept of wholeness.
They basically mean to be made sound, whole, or wholesome.
One word was used as an adjective, as when Jesus visibly restored a person to "health," or when he healed the man with
the withered hand (Matt. 12:13).

John and Matthew use the same word in the incident when
Jesus encounters the paralyzed man at the pool with five por-
ticoes at Beth-zatha. The man had been ill for thirty-eight
years. Jesus asks him if he wanted to be healed, or "become
whole" (John 5:6). The man responded to Jesus and "was
healed, and he took up his pallet and walked" (v. 9). The word
is used again in v. 11 ("The man who *healed* me . . .") and v.
14 ("See, you are *well!*). Luke and Mark chose another word
which meant "sound" or "healthy" (see Luke 5:31; 7:10; 15:27;
Mark 5:34).

In each case, these are incidents that have to do with healing
or restoring to wholeness. Jesus' goal seems to be the health,
the wholeness, of the person. (See also Matt. 9:21f.; 9:12.)

The words also relate to a Biblical concept of salvation.
Wholeness and salvation were similar Biblical concepts. At
Jesus' word people were restored visibly to health. There is an
understanding implied of being "gathered together," becoming "unfragmented." One was "whole" by what Christ did for
the person. Such an understanding did not imply any require-
ment of marriage. One could be single and whole.

The church needs to take another look at the Biblical
meaning of wholeness. If Christ does restore us to wholeness,
then the basis of such wholeness is upon what God does for
us. Wholeness is an act of grace. It is not something we do.
As an act of grace, it is independent of our reliance upon

human institutions for a sense of worth and being.

To gain a sense of wholeness and worth is important for every human being. Our tendency is to attach such worth upon human accomplishments or "works." Thus, one can feel "righteous" about being married. In II Cor. 5:16–17, Paul contends that our full humanity rests in what God has done in Christ. We are a new creation, by the grace of God.

If we say that a person is not whole unless he or she is married, then we may have forsaken an important Biblical affirmation about the meaning of personhood. Single people, as well as married people, need to be helped to find themselves as whole persons, created and redeemed by God.

Friendship

Jesus' basis for his own relationships was not marriage but friendship. There exists, as has been mentioned, no Christian imperative to be married as soon as one can, or to prefer marriage over singleness as a more whole or wholesome situation. Scripture has a good deal to teach us about developing a Christian single adult life-style. A concept of friendship which we see implicitly in Jesus' life-style may be one starting point.

According to Gen. 2:18, it is not good for a person to be alone, to exist in isolation. However, it was not marriage which is seen as the development of mature personhood, but rather learning to live in intimacy with another or others. "Intimacy is 'the need to be known.' . . .'Intimacy means being fully at home with someone. Home is not a place. It is where I am fully known and loved and received just as I am. . . . Only trusted love can give such intimacy.' "[17]

One potential arena for such intimacy for the single adult is friendship. Jesus gives us a clue about friendship. The friend is one who is close or well known, as in Luke 12:4, where Jesus says to his followers, "I tell you, my friends . . ."

The Old Testament root for the word suggests "neighbor" (see Lev. 19:18) or close companionship (as in Deut. 13:6 or Prov. 18:24). The term was also used to denote a relationship between God and humans (Isa. 41:8; James 2:23). But the primary use of the word was applied most frequently to human friendships.

> The Old Testament contains one of the finest instances of friendship. In the final strophe of David's lament for Saul and Jonathan we read: "I am distressed for thee, my *brother* Jonathan . . . " (2 Samuel 1:26).
> The story that ends with the lament is itself a song of praise of friendship. It is said of the two friends in I Samuel 18:1, 3 that "they loved one another as their own life."[18]

In the New Testament, Jesus refers to "our friend Lazarus" (John 11:11). He tells his disciples in three successive verses in John's Gospel:

> Greater love has no man than this, that a man lay down his life for his *friends.* (John 15:13)
> You are *my friends* if you do what I command you. (v. 14)
> No longer do I call you servants . . . ; but I have called you *friends.* (v. 15)

In Luke 12:4, Jesus says, "I tell you, my friends, do not fear."

Many of Jesus' parables and teachings were characterized by a human response of friendship. In Luke, ch. 15, all three parables note that it is friends who are brought together to rejoice. When the elder brother returns home and hears of the feast being given for his prodigal brother, he at once thinks of his friends and the party he missed having (Luke 15:29).

Friendship and table fellowship are correlative in Jesus' life and teachings. He is accused of being "a friend of tax collectors and sinners" (see Matt. 11:19; Luke 7:34). In Luke 14:10, we get the implication that God is both the Lord and the Host at the eschatological banquet who elevates his friends.

Jesus follows this parable by directing his followers' concern not at friendship but at that wall of exclusiveness which any friendship or love can erect, and of which all groups at times have been guilty. (See Luke 14:12–13; and compare with Matt. 5:43–47.) In Matt. 5:43–47, Jesus seems to be calling people to a deeper level of human relationship, one that involves sacrificial love and a friendship that bridges traditional barriers. Culturally defined barriers are not to be a hindrance for his followers. No one need be excluded from the realm of friendship.

The demand that friendship involves a commitment that is sacrificial finds its expression in John 15:12, where Jesus explains that his disciples should be prepared to give their lives for their friends, as he would eventually do. Thus, they would show themselves to be his friends, loving as he did. The saying about supreme love (v. 13) is to apply to the disciples as it does to Jesus.

Jesus demonstrated a compassion for sinners and was loved by them in return, as is shown in Luke 7:37–50, by the washing of his feet, the kiss of friendship, and the anointing with costly ointment. Those who shared in his deep concerns, who listened to his teachings, who agonized over his impending crisis, proved themselves as friends at such a time. They began to find a relationship with Christ as a deep friend.

John's writings describe this relationship between Jesus and his followers as being distinctive. Yet there was an awareness of it not being a friendship between equals. Jesus was still Lord. Yet, such a friendship "was the free choice of the Lord by which he raised his servants to the status of friends. It was not a friendship between equals. Alway he remained Lord."[19]

Jesus' style was an inclusive one in which his love reached out to all. Those who were excluded were only those who excluded themselves. And such people were usually threatened by the inclusiveness of Jesus' friendship with people whom they had managed to exclude. Jesus seemed to revile such exclusiveness as in Matt., ch. 11, when he used the example of John the Baptist being criticized for his forthright preaching and unorthodox style. When Jesus quotes a criticism he had heard about himself: "Behold, a glutton and a drunkard, a friend of tax collectors and sinners!" (Matt. 11:19).

The primitive community saw concealed in the reviling of Jesus the insight that his love for sinners is an enacted parable expressing his message that God makes himself the Friend of sinners.

Jesus' willingness to be a friend to those who were excluded or alone was a model of God's love for all to see, especially the self-righteous. It was, in part, what intensified the opposition to him. Friendship was also an important ingredient in the life of the early church (Acts 10:24; 19:31). Paul chose to fill his life with a variety of friends. He traveled with Barnabas, with young Timothy and John Mark, and with Luke, the physician. He lived for periods of time with Lydia, Priscilla, and Aquila. His words of warmest commendation were for some of his male friends (Eph. 6:21; Col. 4:9; Philemon 24) and his female friends (Rom. 16:2, 7, 12, 15; Phil. 4:3; Col. 4:15).

Many of these persons may have been for Paul what the Celtic Christians of more than a millennium ago spoke of as "a soul-friend" *(amnchara),*[20] or the modern black movement described as a soul brother. These were people who shared their faith and their relationship to Jesus. They were "fellow believers." It was the same kind of supportive sharing as expressed by the author of III John to his readers: "Peace be to you. The friends greet you. Greet the friends, every one of them" (III John 15).

The church can begin to look afresh at the Biblical meaning of friendship. There is strong Biblical material that has not been interpreted adequately to help people understand the potential and worth of human friendship.

For the single adult, as well as for other adults, there can be an encouragement toward cultivating good friendships. I found that many singles tend to look to friendships as a means of finding human community. A good friend may often be the visible presence of such a community. The church could do more to help people find and cultivate friendships that are more fulfilling and meaningful.

A Supportive Community

Single adults need a sense of being a part of a supportive, caring community. A sense of community has deep roots Biblically. The earliest forms of Judaism spring from a sense of community which people shared as they tried to live out a common faith in a covenant-making God. That covenant even took on the form of Law, as the faith community ordered itself to care for all in the covenant community. The Mosaic Law included "words" or commands which took into account mutual support and concern:

> Honor your father and your mother. . . . You shall not kill
> . . . commit adultery . . . steal . . . bear false witness against your
> neighbor . . . covet your neighbor's house . . . or anything that
> is your neighbor's. (Ex. 20:12–17)

The Law seemed to be concerned that a faith in a covenant-keeping God involved caring about the welfare of one's neighbor, family, and property. When this sense of supportive community began to erode, through lack of concern, or by exploitation, indifference, etc., the prophets spoke loudly against such injustice. (Cf. Jer. 9:3–6; Hos. 12:7–9; Micah 6:6–8; Isa. 59:1–8.)

In the New Testament, we see Jesus calling people to follow him. He offered his love to all. Those who responded to that love found they were called to be a supportive community, grounded in his love. Jesus expected them to be such a community. "By this all men will know that you are my disciples, if you have love for one another" (John 13:35). Jesus expected his followers to care for one another. Such people soon found that a sense of community began to be expressed as they responded to Christ's love for each of them. As Dietrich Bonhoeffer once described: "Our community with one another consists solely in what Christ has done to both of us."[21]

Those who were cared for by Christ began to care for one another. They were bound by his caring. It was this atmosphere of open support which began to characterize the life of the early church. It was a communion or fellowship, involving a fellowship not only between God and his people but also among the people. Without compromising the completeness of Christ's Lordship, or modifying the fundamental truth that the whole relationship is based on God's sovereign grace, close fellowship developed. The people understood that they were called into existence by a covenant-keeping God. Trusting in God's sovereignty, they then began to shape their life together into a supportive community. They prayed for one another (see Phil. 1:3–4; I Cor. 1:4; Acts 2:42), offered mutual support when a need arose (see I Cor. 16:1–2; II Cor. 8:3; Rom. 12:13; 15:26), and shared in mutual ministry.

Acts 2:42 describes some of the life of this early Christian community: they devoted themselves to the apostles' teaching and fellowship, to the breaking of bread and prayers. There was a mutual sharing (Acts 4:32 to 5:10). "There was not a needy person among them" (Acts 4:34). In those early days, this system enabled the community to care for one another's needs, to "bear one another's burdens, and so fulfil the law of Christ" (Gal. 6:2).

Luke characteristically described the life of this early community. As his Gospel notes, Jesus cared for those who were overlooked by the general establishment. For Luke, offenses against the common life are directed against the Holy Spirit (Acts 5:3, 9). Paul also criticized those who come to share in sacramental communion yet who remained insensitive to the needs of those in the community (I Cor. 11:19–22). Paul's concept of Christian community grew out of his belief that the church is the body of Christ. The Christian community is a body of diverse persons, indwelt and united by the Spirit. In I Cor., ch. 12, Paul describes that body as having "many members" (vs. 12, 14), yet united by the Spirit "for the common good" (v. 7). One part cannot say to another part that it is not needed. Each part is important for the proper functioning of the body. In this same chapter, Paul deals with the importance of gifts of the Spirit. He notes that there are "varieties of gifts, but the same Spirit" (v. 4). Part of the task of the supportive community is to help persons realize their God-given gifts, their uniqueness, and to call these forth for ministry to others. Mutual care and support is important and essential in such a process.

Worship is one context for supportive community to develop, called by God. It is essential as persons are enabled to respond to God's call for their commitment. Not only does the good news of God's love offer forgiveness and healing, but it also calls forth a sense of okayness that comes from knowing one is loved and restored to wholeness. The Sacraments of Baptism and Communion are visible, liturgical expressions of that supportive community. As "outward signs of an inward grace" they represent incorporation into, and ongoing care within that community. Both Sacraments are visible expressions of that community, called by God, and sustained by Christ through the working of the Spirit.

Baptism expresses one's ingrafting into the covenant community, as an expression of grace and forgiveness. As such, it demonstrates "the new creation," spoken of by Paul in II Cor.

5:17, "the old has passed away, behold, the new has come." It "marks a new beginning of participation in Christ's ministry for all people."[22]

Communion is a liturgical expression of "the fellowship of believers with their Lord and with one another."[23] It is an ongoing reminder of the gathered community which is gathered, fed, redeemed, renewed, sent forth in ministry. At the Lord's Table all who confess Christ are welcome and fed. Here, "there is neither Jew nor Greek, there is neither slave nor free, there is neither male nor female" (Gal. 3:28), there is neither married nor single, for all are one in Christ.

It is the community of faith which continues to share the sacrament of renewal in Christ. As a sign of the risen Christ, the breaking of bread can speak to the brokenness of human life and its relationships. The risen Lord is proclaimed and present.

In worship, the gathered community brings its world. Worship affirms the presence and Lordship of Christ in such a world. An "incarnational" theology enables us to face our human relationships with courage and hope. There is also a call to commitment, to trust, and to ministry. Jesus called people to leave everything and to follow him. (See Matt. 19:27; Luke 18:29–30.) Discipleship is an individual call and response that finds meaning and direction in community.

As Dietrich Bonhoeffer notes:

> Though we all have to enter upon discipleship alone, we do not remain alone. If we take Him [Jesus] at His word and dare to become individuals, our reward is the fellowship of the Church. Here is a visible brotherhood [and sisterhood] to compensate a hundredfold for all we have lost.[24]

Commenting on the church community described in Matt. 19:27 and Luke 18:29, Linda LeSourd notes:

Unfortunately, few modern church fellowships exemplify this kind of dedication and commitment. As a result, Christians hungering for a shared life with other believers are often dissatisfied with the church. This is especially true for singles lacking the fullness of a family life. Few of them realize how far such a caring community would go toward meeting deep needs they have previously associated with marriage.[25]

She goes on to point out that it takes time to build such a community and most churches do not feel called to pursue such a task.

Yet there are many aspects of genuine Christian community which can be incorporated into the local church right now. Diversity, commitment, love and deep relationships are four such characteristics which are especially important to the single woman [person].[26]

Christian community is a gift of God which we cannot claim. It is, as Bonhoeffer states, "a reality created by God in Christ in which we may participate."[27] Thus, "to exclude the weak and insignificant, the seemingly useless people, from a Christian community may actually mean the exclusion of Christ."[28]

The church can be a supportive community, created by God, where the Spirit moves freely, calling forth and using the unique gifts of each person, drawing others into its life, worship, and ministry. Drawing its style from the Christ, it can call persons to wholeness and provide friendships which are affirming and nonexploitive.

The Confession of 1967 of The United Presbyterian Church U.S.A. expresses the tone of this belief as it speaks about some of the ways in which the Christian life takes shape:

The new life takes shape in a community in which men [people] know that God loves and accepts them in spite of what they are. They therefore accept themselves and love others, knowing that no man [one] has any ground on which to stand except God's grace.[29]

Operating from an inclusive style, the church can provide a place where persons, single and married, can gather for worship, study, and ministry. Very few ongoing institutions in society have this potential for calling forth humans into wholeness and freedom. The challenge is put to the church.

The Word of God tells us that each of us is complete in Christ (Col. 2:10). "*Complete* means 'lacking in nothing . . . full . . . whole . . . inclusion of all that is needed for perfection or fulfillment.' "[30]

Jesus called people to freedom, to personhood, to community. He offered friendship and relationship within a supportive fellowship. "When people are free for personhood, to trust, and for community, free to develop our unlimited potential and to value each other for who we are and who we are becoming—then, we will be 'free indeed.' "[31]

SUMMARY

Many single adults, some of whom are Christian, are searching today for new forms, new contexts, new ways in which they can find and express their wholeness as single persons. They are searching for a sense of wholeness that both affirms their singleness and gives them a sense of participation within the human community.

The church faces a unique challenge in working with single adults in that process. To do that, however, the church needs to rethink its Biblical and theological roots for developing a perspective on singleness. Previously, it was difficult to affirm singleness as a valid life-style because of some of the Biblical, cultural emphases upon marriage, family, procreation, etc. Marriage and procreation have, at times, been essential to support the clan, the tribe, the nation. Divorce was not an acceptable reality because it countered such an emphasis.

Yet, it was Christianity that made the single life possible. It was Christianity that substituted the family of faith for the family of blood. Jesus said that those who were his family were those who did the will of God (Matt. 12:50).

It is time that the church faces the reality of single adulthood and lets the Scriptures speak in a fresh way. Possible interrelated new starting points for such an affirmation of singleness might be a reunderstanding of the message of wholeness in Christ, the Biblical meaning and importance of friendship, and the reality of a supportive community.

Jesus called and restored people to wholeness. He put them into a relationship with one another and called them his friends. This sense of gathering enabled the community of faith to be an inclusive reality for a variety of persons. Marriage was not a prerequisite to discipleship. Somehow, the early church experienced itself as a body in Christ. Each person was affirmed for his or her uniqueness and called to express that uniqueness through the realization and use of God-given gifts. These gifts were of value to the community of faith.

Today, single adults search for a sense of wholeness, of singleness that is not "less than whole." They affirm the value of friends and often find that a variety of friends provides a supportive community that is vital to their well-being. Other singles still search without satisfaction. Often broken and fragmented from an experience of divorce, separation, grief, etc., many singles yearn for people who can help them rebuild again. Old friends may no longer relate to them. Some look to the church and find they are not understood or heard. And they wait for an indication from the church that it is okay to be single.

The church must listen to the concerns of singles, and to the ways in which God may be speaking today through such persons. It must listen to the Scriptures in a new way, trusting that God's Spirit will guide it into new directions for understanding and affirming singles. Such an affirmation can be developed alongside of a legitimate concern for the quality and integrity of marriage. In fact, a sound appreciation of singleness may also help provide a more solid approach to the institution of marriage. Then the church needs to move toward finding ways to minister to and with single adults. Adequate forms can emerge out of a theological base that affirms the validity of being both human and single.

6

WHAT FORM
SHALL A SINGLES MINISTRY TAKE?

(A LOOK AT SOME OPTIONS)

THE CHURCH tries to minister to people in groups (junior highs, couples, church officers, etc.). But singles are not easy to group. They are diverse. Some singles have little interest in attending "singles groups." Others want a group in which to participate.

Let's look at some possible groups and other options for the church's ministry to single adults.

TYPES OF GROUPS

Ministries among single adults come in all sizes, shapes, and perspectives. No one size or shape can fit every situation.

In his book *A Pew for One, Please,* William Lyon provides a helpful description of four basic types of singles groups: the church-sponsored singles group (CSSG), the church-related singles group (CRSG), the church-dominated singles group (CDSG), and the church-integrated singles group (CISG).

The church-sponsored singles group (CSSG) "gives very little evidence that religious concepts or practices influence the group's functioning."[1] The meetings of such groups are primarily social in nature. Membership frequently consists of "a core of regulars, augmented by a large number of occasional attenders."[2] While such groups may not provide much spiritual content for participants, they do enable singles, particularly women, to meet other singles in a more trusting atmosphere.

Socialization in such CSSGs usually "follows the pattern of social dating: introductions, chatting, refreshments, chatting, a touch of serious talk, dancing, chatting, and promises to meet again."[3]

Such groups most frequently lack any element of spiritual depth. The stress on socialization tends to draw "body shoppers," those who are date or mate hunting. The church sponsoring body may provide its facility for use, but very little supervision beyond that point. These groups cost the church very little in terms of personnel, money, or time.

An exception would be an organization like the Solo Center in Seattle. Originally sponsored by the Unitarian Church, the Solo Center describes itself as "a nonprofit, nondenominational center for single adults in transition."[4] Solo Center operates out of a house that has been renovated to accompany many rap groups and small seminars. It houses office space for a full-time director and support staff. The center maintains a loose relationship to its original sponsoring body, and maintains an almost nonexistent religious emphasis. A board of directors directs its wide variety of activities. Drawing from community and statewide leadership, Solo Center offers a full weekly program of seminars, classes, lectures, workshops, and social activities for single adults of all ages and categories. A newspaper is published monthly as a resource for singles in the metropolitan area. Circulated to more than eleven thousand single adults, the *Solo Center News* provides a valuable service, publicizing area events, and articles of interest.

The second type is the church-related singles group (CRSG). There is a stronger tie between the sponsoring body and the singles group. Lyon cites two examples of thriving CRSGs, both of which have paid staff and more than one hundred members. One example is a singles group from the massive ten-thousand-member Garden Grove Community Church. This church separates its singles by age: Pacesetters (20s), Innovators (30s), Motivators (40s), and Lamplighters (over 50). Over eighty-five percent of the Innovators are formerly married. Activities include a heavy social schedule, Bible study, and worship. The administrative structure is highly organized. All elected officers are required to be members of the Community Church. Outside groups are prevented from taking over the program's direction. The sponsoring church holds a tight reign on the program.

Such CRSGs tend to have a clear purpose, and attract a rather heterogeneous membership. There are weaknesses. They may attract large numbers of visitors, many of whom will not return. Group officers tend to run the program for the participants rather than with them.

The danger in the highly successful CRSG is to focus on statistical success rather than on individual spiritual-emotional growth, or *"quantity* at the expense of *quality."*[5] Lyon questions to what extent the singles group is a front for the church with which it is affiliated.

The third category is the church-dominated singles group (CDSG). In this group,

> the purpose, program, and philosophy of that church's program is not to minister to single persons in terms of those problems and needs that are unique to them as *singles* but, rather, to use the singles' program as but one more technique for bringing people into the church.[6]

This highlights one reason why a church needs to be aware of its motives for developing a singles ministry.

Sometimes a church can dominate one of its groups by depriving it of a sense of identity. Such domination may be an evidence of giving only lip service to the purpose for such a group to deal with the needs of single persons.

Usually the leadership comes from a core of church faithfuls, often older in age. They may readily express concern, friendliness, and affection, though not necessarily deep sharing. There may be a strong ministry to "spiritual needs" to "the exclusion of other needs, such as the psychological, emotional, recreational-social, educational, and practical problems of divorce and living alone."[7] There is often heavy emphasis upon repentance and salvation, yet very little on personal growth, interpersonal relations, or the uniqueness of their single state. This style of singles group is frequently found in fundamentalist, evangelical, and charismatic churches.

The fourth category is the church-integrated singles group (CISG). This group is given the assistance, respect, and importance accorded to other groups in the church. Group members tend to be active participants in other church activities. There is interpersonal experience that tends to foster trust, sharing, affection, support, and self-growth. There is an atmosphere of openness, members seem honest with one another, enjoy being together, and reach out readily to newcomers.

Some of the disadvantages of the CISG include: many newcomers do not fit in comfortably, narrowness and exclusion can easily set in, and members may never really have to know or relate to each other in "real life."[8] Also, such groups might not be appropriate for persons who are not committed or even interested in becoming heavily involved in a particular church. Because a church-integrated singles group encourages a close interaction with its church prospective membership, a single person who either belongs to another church or who does not yet have an interest in joining *any* may not feel at ease with its emphasis.

Lyon emphasizes, in support of the latter style of singles group, that:

singles' groups can be created as integral parts of the church and still retain the individuality of the persons, the group, and the church. More important, within this kind of group structure the church can become an integral part of the person.[9]

A congregation needs to think through the extent of its commitment to a singles ministry, and what form it wishes its ministry to take. If its concern is primarily for those singles who are within the realm of the congregation's life, then a church-integrated style might be the most natural. As the perimeters expand outward beyond the congregation, such a form may be more difficult. A congregation needs to decide how large a scope of need it is willing to tackle.

Single adults who are within the church should be encouraged to speak up concerning their needs and desires. They are a part of the body of Christ also. They can help shape the body's ministry to other singles by being a part of the decision-making process.

Pastors and decision-making bodies would do well to spend significant time with the singles who are in their congregation as well as community. Probing their felt needs, their experiences as single persons within the congregation and community, matching these data with those found in outside research, can all prove helpful in determining what form a ministry with singles might take.

Once such data are obtained, then some decisions can be made regarding the most appropriate form of ministry.

GENERAL MINISTRIES: ECUMENICAL OR INTERCHURCH?

In larger metropolitan areas, frequently there are congregations large enough to hire staff who can specifically deal with a ministry to single adults. However, many congregations lack funds or personnel for a specialized singles ministry.

Cooperative forms of ministry provide a viable option for the local congregation which might lack resources for carrying out its own ministry to singles. In an age of dwindling economic resources, ecumenical or interchurch efforts have proven to be one viable option in many communities.

Commenting on such efforts, Robert Lyon suggests that "when two or more churches co-sponsor a singles' group, it would be well for them to do so with a church whose values and traditions will not be in conflict with the other church's."[10] Church-sponsored or church-related singles groups do not seem to run as much risk of interchurch conflict as do the church-integrated and church-dominated groups.

However, a congregation that enters into a cooperative form of ministry needs to be willing to sacrifice some of its traditional ways of doing things, as well as its stereotypes of how things ought to be done. New forms of ministry can arise out of cooperative efforts. Where one church enters such conversations with a predetermined set of standards, cooperation may be difficult and hindered.

The value of a cooperative approach can be seen in the sharing of personnel, space, finances, and planning resources. One congregation may be willing to sponsor a singles group, offering its space and personnel, while soliciting support from other congregations.

The North End Tacoma Singles group meets at a Presbyterian Church in Tacoma, Washington. It is more of an ecumenical organization, led by a layperson from the sponsoring church. Other lay leadership is drawn from the participants, many of whom are from other churches. Membership in the group tends to rest heavily on the forty to sixty age bracket, with about fifty participants. Activities are varied, including Bible study, and a heavy emphasis upon social activities. Events are publicized by many of the area churches. Members of the group tend to be familiar with and supportive of one another. This cooperative group would come close to the church-integrated category described earlier. While somewhat limited to an older age bracket, its ministry seems supportive of those who attend.

In the greater Seattle area few churches with fewer than one thousand members are able to sustain strong ministries to single adults. The strongest programs are being carried out by cooperative ministries to specific types of singles. What seems evident is that there are large churches, staffed, and carrying on somewhat active ministries to singles. Then, there are a few isolated efforts by smaller congregations to singles in general. Few cooperative ministries and ministries to singles in general seem to exist, especially among moderate or liberal churches.

One form of cooperative ministry might include the sharing of resources, as well as the sponsorship of occasional retreats and special events. This can provide a valuable supplement and variation from smaller local church efforts.

In a time when great change is occurring within society, there does not seem to be any one form of ministry that "works" in a wide variety of situations. Cooperative ministries may well prove necessary. If these do not take the shape of an actual ministry to singles on a regular basis, they at least can provide an arena for sharing resources, successes and failures, joint program planning, and occasional shared events and personnel.

Special Ministries Related to Need

The most concerted effort in singles ministry in many church bodies is directed toward particular groups of singles. When there is a concentration of a particular category of single adults, such as young singles, or divorcées, or widows, a ministry centering around needs might prove most realistic.

For example, in surveying its own constituency, a congregation, might find there is an unusually high number of divorced persons. Rather than develop a broad singles ministry, a ministry to divorced persons may be considered.

Divorce, as has been indicated, is a painful experience. Women especially find themselves marooned by it. Men also need sensitive pastoral care. Divorced people are often avoided in the church. Yet in every congregation and community, people are getting divorced and seek to rebuild their lives once again.

Britton Wood says:

> The formerly married usually feel out of place in most churches because adequate programming has not developed to meet their needs. . . . The mind-set of the church generally does not consider the formerly married person's situation or feelings. Single adults and married adults have some similar needs but they also have needs that are unique and must be cared for in different ways.[11]

Perhaps one of the most neglected needs in the church is a ministry to couples when they are separated, facing divorce, and making adjustments during the time immediately after a divorce. These are times of intense trauma and emotional upheaval. Some people must go through a divorce or separation with no one to listen, no one to help, no one to be a friend to them.

One author notes that this can often be a time when the local church could do a great deal, yet doesn't.

> There needs to be a change in the attitudes of the staff and church members toward persons who are involved in divorce. Why is it that when there is a death, people rush right in with visits, food, and offers of help? Yet, when a person is facing divorce—the death of a marriage—many people stay away. They don't know what to say, or are afraid of intruding. Yet this

is a time when people are desperately needed. The reassurance that you are still acceptable, not someone undesirable, and that you are worthy of friendship, helps to restore a feeling of self-worth.[12]

The church can provide a supportive, caring ministry to divorced persons. In order to do that, some theological rearranging may need to happen in many congregations. William Lyon calls upon the church "to develop a theology which deals with divorce as a fact of life and recognize divorced persons and one-parent families resulting from divorce as acceptable persons who need love and support."[13]

Britton Wood also urges the church to reconsider its attitude toward divorced persons. Needed are healthier ways to care for persons going through divorce. He suggests that

> a support group in the church for caring, listening and sharing of insights regarding divorce can be most helpful. Such a group can take different forms. It may consist of three to eight formerly married persons who are brought together by the minister or single adult leader.[14]

The church could "assist all formerly married persons with friendships which can give insight regarding finances, all kinds of decision-making, vocational guidance, the process of grief, and spiritual nurturing in the midst of suffering."[15] The church can have employment information for single adults who are between jobs. It can also provide counsel for those who feel they need to change professions. The church could offer opportunities for single parents to have child care in order to attend retreats, lectures, group experiences, or just have some time alone. And it can provide valuable assistance and support to children of divorced parents.

Anne Hagen, writing in *The Lutheran Standard*, suggests some ways concerned Christians can give support to divorced persons: (1) listen, be a supportive listener, (2) don't judge, (3) forgive what seems to be total self-absorption, (4) be innovative, find some ways to include them with other adults socially, and (5) affirm them as individuals, just the way they are. The care of the church community is important at such a time. Divorced persons, as other people, "need to be integrated and accepted into the family of believers."[16]

Garner Scott Odell, while serving in a Presbyterian church in Berkeley, California, developed a model for ministry to divorced persons that centered on two concepts: (1) a loving, supportive community of people with problems related to separation and divorce; (2) a group that would focus on problem-solving rather than on therapy and social contacts. The purpose of this model was "to offer a gathering for people dealing together with the problems and joys surrounding the death of a marital contract."[17] People came from all over the Bay area to participate in such discussions as aloneness, sex, dating, raising children, legal and financial matters. In his research, he found that there were not enough separated or divorced people within each church to form a special ministry in each congregation.

A ministry to divorced persons may be carried out on a larger, more ecumenical scale. In Seattle, for instance, Divorce Lifeline, a group counseling program for the separated and divorced, is sponsored by the Presbyterian Counseling Service. The program originated in 1967 at a Presbyterian church. A layperson who was going through a divorce felt he needed a supportive group. He gathered other divorced persons, and the group formed, under the directorship of Rev. Neal Kuyper. The program expanded in its scope, adding more facilitators of small groups as well as professional staff. It extended into five other Washington communities and two out-of-state communities.

Divorce Lifeline and its Tacoma counterpart, Divorce Outreach, are therapy programs that offer supportive guidance by professional group leaders. They seek to help each person achieve personal growth and readjustment through group interaction. The program is interdenominational. Persons who are considering, going through, or already are divorced, may participate in the six- to eight-week process at fees based on ability to pay.

Such ministries are evidence that the church can creatively provide a solid and sensitive program for single persons. The same could be done with other categories of singles. In Seattle, for instance, a Single Parent Family Program has been formed. It is sponsored by the Puget Counseling Center and the Pastoral Care Committee of the Church Council of Greater Seattle. This educational/mental health program for single parents and families provides retreats, workshops, classes, and counseling.

Persons who are single by death can turn to Widowed Lifeline, a therapy-oriented group designed to help widows and widowers adjust and grow in a Christian context. This program is also sponsored by the Presbyterian Counseling Service and receives ecumenical support.

The church in the greater Seattle area has demonstrated a sensitivity to the large number of single adults in the surrounding population. While few churches have been able to develop a strong ministry with singles, working cooperatively, they seem to have put their concerns into action. Several of the particular ministries mentioned are providing solid forms of caring to singles. Yet much more could be done. Many local churches never publicize the area services that are offered to singles, much less provide satisfying outlets for their own singles. Many pastors either are not aware of such ministries or do not bother to support them. In some communities, the best service a church could offer would be to publicize good existing opportunities for singles in the wider community.

THE NONGROUP MINISTRY

It would be easy to assume that the only way to provide a ministry for single adults would be to form a singles group. This is a trap that many local churches fall into. If they are not able to get a group going successfully, they often conclude there is not much that can be done with singles.

There are alternatives to singles groups open to churches that want to reach out to single adults in meaningful and helpful ways. A nongroup singles ministry can occur through churches and groups of churches that are willing to think creatively.

I was able to participate with a group of single adults in the formation of a singles center. This was the result of several months of conversation with area single adults from churches, singles groups, the YMCA and YWCA, and interested community singles. Through the Associated Ministries of Tacoma-Pierce County, an open meeting was called for people who were concerned about the needs of Christian singles in Pierce County.

Over forty persons attended the initial meeting. Interest was high in surveying what services and programs were available in the area for single adults, and what was lacking. It was concluded, after research, that most needed were: (1) a means of communication to singles that would tell about all the groups and services available and (2) a place where singles could meet for informal recreation, counseling, workshops, and mutual support. A steering committee was established for the purpose of pursuing this action.

Eventually an organization was formed and bylaws were adopted. The purpose, as stated in the bylaws, was

> to serve the needs of adult singles in Pierce County by providing information about and referral to existing singles' groups, pro-

viding an informal gathering place for singles, a center for counseling and workshops and other appropriate activities.[18]

The group is currently providing information of singles
activities in the area, as well as pursuing its goal of establishing a place where singles can gather. It is an example
of how the church can serve the larger community as
an enabler for responsible action. Rather than the formation of new groups, which would have only been repe-
titious, what was needed was a nongroup coordinating ministry.

Other nongroup options are possible. Consciousness-raising certainly is a necessary action in most churches. "Our
most important task, both as congregations and as individuals, is to enlarge our view about the single person in the
church."[19] Providing opportunities for single and married
persons to share one another's concerns is an important
part of any consciousness-raising process. The church could
offer classes, formal and informal, designed to serve adults
who are single. Single persons in the congregation or community could be utilized as leaders. Social programs and
special projects could be provided for single and married
persons to explore together. Church libraries could acquire
books that deal responsibly with singleness, its problems,
potential, and challenges. Resources for those who are sepa-
rating, facing divorce, widowed, or single parents could be
provided. Smaller churches might provide a cooperative
lending library of resources. Sermons, possibly in the nature
of a dialogue, could deal with the needs of single adults.

Consciousness-raising certainly involves language. Just as the
church has had to reevaluate its use of sexist terminology, so
also family-oriented language needs to be looked at, particularly
when it excludes those who are single.

Instead of "single," we say "unmarried," which implies that being married is the normal state. Sexism is also part of our picture of the single person. Thus a woman who reaches a certain age without marrying is still described as an "old maid," while for the single man the term "bachelor" is less often used and rarely in a derogatory sense.[20]

Speaking from "a church frame of reference," Britton Wood suggests some other consciousness-raising ways the church can serve single persons, by:

1. Providing channels for healthy singles' relationships.
2. Reconsidering its attitude toward divorced persons.
3. Assisting the formerly married to find friendships that will offer spiritual nurture.
4. Recognizing various levels of personal and spiritual development among singles.
5. Recognizing singles' participation in the church and commending them.
6. Recognizing the importance of "the family of God" in the life of the singles.[21]

It might be easier to think of constructive ways for raising the consciousness of church members toward singles in the church than to develop an awareness of those single persons who are apart from the church. These people need to be listened to and ministered unto also. Many of them left the church because they did not sense they were heard or needed. Some of them carry a sense of guilt, of failure, of aimlessness. They grapple with difficult questions about sexuality, divorce, living together, commitment, and so on.

A congregation that understands the value of singleness, and affirms those persons who are single, as well as those who are married, can have an important ministry of wholeness and healing. It will find single adults who bring time, energy, support, and creativity. It will find single persons who are willing to assume responsible leadership. There are many singles who want to be involved in the total church community where they can enjoy the diversity of the whole body of Christ.

In its report to the Church Council of Greater Seattle the singles task force included the following recommendation for what the church can do in its ministry to single adults:

> It is highly recommended that individual congregations provide pastoral care to singles by developing an outreach for their distinct needs, not simply at the times of crisis.
>
> However, singles should not be forever "singled out" for still another workshop on divorce, custody, visitation rights, dating, and remarriage. Nor should they be restricted "to their own kind." The church is a family and "family" means love and community. Everyone is looking for love and wholeness; no one can find it in isolation.[22]

Some Alternative Forms of Ministry

Some churches, in developing a ministry with singles, will choose to form singles groups. Such groups may be for singles in general, or they may be directed toward a specific category of single (young, widowed, divorced). Some will choose an ecumenical or cooperative ministry.

There are other alternatives to these approaches which might be explored. These may not "work" in some congregations. They may be more natural in certain settings. In any case, the church should give serious consideration to developing alternatives to its traditional group pattern of ministry to singles.

Extended Families

Because of increased mobility in American culture few people remain in close proximity to those relatives who comprise the nuclear family. In older times, as well as in many other cultures, one lived a lifetime within the bounds of an extended family. There were grandparents, aunts and uncles, cousins, relatives who were never married, as well as widows and widowers. Children were able to grow up having "significant other" adults, beyond their parents, with whom to talk and spend time. But such relationships are scarce in this age of rapid mobility, corporation control, and tentative commitments. Because of a lack of "rootage" many people grow up without much sense of identity or family solidarity.

Single adults often get the short end of this characteristic of our culture. A widower may be employed in a city far away from his hometown or children. A divorcée may live with her children in a city, or suburb, unable to spend time with parents or relatives. A young man or woman, never married, may be transferred out of the region, beyond all family ties.

A sense of family may be hard to realize for such persons. Yet a sense of family is important for all persons, whether single or married.

The church can be one arena where that sense of family can be cultivated. Experiments in extended family relationships may be one important direction to move as an alternative form of ministry.

John Yoder suggests an extended family structure as one positive opportunity for the church to provide in supporting the dignity of singleness.

> We need to re-create extended family structures in which the single person can be at home socially, economically, in family prayer and household chores.
>
> The pattern of the extended family could be used . . . to provide for every single person a place to be the elder brother or sister, aunt or uncle in some family, with great freedom to drop in or perhaps preferably sharing the residence, finding both security and liberty.[23]

Anthropologist Margaret Mead is quoted by author Lynn Caine:

> I think that family living will become increasingly narrow, cramped, and frustrating unless married couples open the doors of their homes and bring some singles into their lives. Opening the doors of friendship to the widowed, the divorced, and the never-married would bring a family blessed relief from the daily repetition of the same themes and the same controversies through the welcome diversity of other views and other interests.[24]

The church could provide opportunity for a variety of persons to enter into an extended family covenant for a given time. It might be possible for a group of persons who are not related to combine into an extended family agreement, relating to each other in roles analogous to family roles, e.g., grandparent–grandchild, cousin–aunt. There can, and probably should be, a variation in age. The people need not share the same household, but may agree to spend occasional weekends together, or a vacation or a holiday. They might select outings to share, or meals after church. Children might be invited to spend the weekend with "grandmother," thus freeing the single parent or parents to get away. There can be many variations in style.

Carole Klein observes that "children of single parents are unusually open to an extended idea of family."[25]

The Presbyterian-related Community for Christian Celebration, in Olympia, Washington, has included extended family opportunities in its creative and varied program. In a congregation of fewer than one hundred members, there are several extended family contracts, many of which are convened by singles. These groups include married persons and their children. According to Pastor Jim Symons, "this is a good way to include everyone in relatively intimate support networks, while at the same time acting in mission on various projects with the Community for Christian Celebration and in the larger community."[26]

On a scale of 1–5, Pastor Symons rates the ministry of his congregation with single adults at 5 (very satisfactory). The extended family opportunity is one of several ways in which single adults are incorporated into the life and ministry of that church.

A congregation in the East provides an extended family experience of worship, fellowship, and learning. Participants include: one couple with three teen-agers, one couple with three elementary-age children, two retired widowers, a single woman with two preschoolers, and a couple with two preschoolers. The group meets one Sunday night a month for a potluck supper, family worship or experiential education, a break to take children home to bed, followed by an adult discussion. The time span is three and one half hours.[27]

Problems for the group include: difficulty in including new members after a certain size was reached, including persons living outside the locality, and "what to do after four years." Some time of closure might be included in an extended family contract.

Donald Allen, in *Barefoot in the Church*, relates an extended family benefit that came out of a house church experience:

> One emerging dimension in the quest for community is the willingness of so many, particularly young adults, to change the narrow meaning of "family." In the past the term referred chiefly to the primary family tree, including all the cousins and half-sisters for at least four generations. In our own day the "family" often means the single household across the street whom we see going to work and school each morning. Now the word "family" may mean the number of friends who make up our boundary of extreme openness, trust and commitment to a common goal.[28]

Christian Communal Arrangements

The communal movement has a rather spotty history. It reached a peak in America in 1800–1860. Then, according to William Kephart,

> in the late 1960s, communalism underwent a rebirth. Communes of all sizes, shapes, and descriptions seemed to sprout overnight. Some were urban, some rural. Some were secular, others religious. Some shared sex, others did not. Many were frankly escapist in nature, and most seemed to appeal to the younger age groups.[29]

There are different kinds of communes. There are retreat communes, which seek withdrawal from society. And there are service communes, which seek engagement and involvement, often settling in cities.

The communal movement of the 1960's seems to have run its course. Some communes have survived and done well. Others could not maintain their original intent or zeal. Many disbanded because their participants left, disillusioned by their unmet utopian dreams. There might still be opportunities which can emerge, and which provide unique opportunities for interdependent communities.

One possibility might include communal households. John Yoder proposes the possibility of a household of mixed singles. This might include mixed singles and childless couples, "still differing from the 'extended family' in that the absence of children would facilitate certain other kinds of community life focus."[30] Yoder also suggests the possibility of sexually segregated communes of single persons, "supporting one another in a life-style of consecrated singleness. The absence of members of the other sex will encourage the development of more gifts and roles among the members of the group."[31]

Gray Panther activist Maggie Kuhn suggests the possibility of intergenerational communal homes. Encouraging widows "who live alone in their large homes" to open up their places to college or single adults, Ms. Kuhn notes that such arrangements might teach "a new kind of interdependence."[32] Space could be used in new ways, resources shared, and a new approach to common tasks learned.

Churches could help people experiment with the stewardship of property and resources, as well as provide some creative extended family arrangements. Elderly people would not have to live in fear of their safety in a large, empty house, nor eat alone.

Worship/Celebrations and Singles

Biblical faith witnesses that we are a creation of God. Our worship can be a celebration of that creation, recognizing the reality of human sinfulness and divine forgiveness. It can be an experience where every aspect of human life is brought to, or confronted by, the creative, forgiving, restoring fullness of God's love. In worship God's initiating grace and human response to that grace find focus. A logical response is commitment and service. Worship, then, ought to focus on God's power and grace, as it confronts every dimension of daily living.

In worship, individuals are drawn, by a common response to God's love, toward community and ministry together. As a person experiences forgiveness and wholeness, there is a common bond with others as servants and friends in Christ. The direction from worship is toward others, toward a hurting world. "Significant corporate worship occurs primarily, if not exclusively, in those communities that have shared deeply together."[33]

If Allen's statement is on target, then one prerequisite of corporate worship is a sense of supportive community. One wonders how much real worship occurs where there is no sense of such community.

For the single adult who comes to a local church for worship, but who does not feel welcome or understood as a person, the experience of corporate worship may be difficult. If the sermons, language, hymns, and style of the service are directed toward families, serious limitations may be put on the participation and response of single adults.

As has been mentioned, the single adult often feels isolated and uncomfortable in church. While there may be resources and groups available in a community for singles, providing therapy, support, and social opportunities, the single may feel excluded when it comes to corporate worship within the body of Christ.

There are ways in which a local church can be more inclusive of singles in corporate worship. Sermons can include illustrations drawn from single life, or deal with topics common to singles. Singles can be invited to participate in dialogues, as well as assist in lay leadership. Prayers may include intercessions for those who experience divorce, grief, transition, and other particular joys and challenges. Hymns and anthems can be adapted in their language.

Those who experience grief over death are frequently "remembered" in corporate worship. Seldom included are those who are in the grief process of separation or divorce. The church participates joyfully in the marriage of two persons, but it is silent when that marriage bond is broken or ended. The United Methodist Church recently produced a ceremony of divorce that can be a public way of lending support to a person or a couple who is divorcing.[34]

The Baptism of infants, as well as of adults, is a corporate recognition of entrance into the household of faith. In the Presbyterian tradition, the congregation accepts a responsibility for nurture and support of the child as well as of the parents. Baptism is an expression that we are "members one of another" (Rom. 12:5). To follow through with the implications of promises made at Baptism is a challenge constantly facing the church. There are applications for single adults. Baptized children of single parents are a responsibility of the household of faith, as are the single parents. Sensitive ways of caring might be explored by congregations that are desirous of "putting flesh" to their promises.

The church ought to rethink its stance on remarriage. Many congregations, or at least pastors, do not demonstrate acceptance of the remarriage of divorced persons. The Biblical interpretation is that a person who remarries commits "adultery" (Matt. 19:9; I Cor. 7:11). By not rethinking its stance on remarriage, in a day when divorce—and remarriage—figures are high, the church displays a rigid lack of understanding and care. By not dealing with remarriage, the church indicates a lack of acceptance of the previously married single person. It is almost as if the church does not forgive the person for being single.

With rethinking on remarriage might come worship expressions that celebrate singleness. In its recognition of divorce, as well as of remarriage, the church could help single persons to move toward an affirmation and understanding of their singleness.

Another possible direction related to single adults and worship might be the development of a community for singles centering around worship and celebration. Such an ingredient is often lacking in many communities, particularly for those singles of less conservative Christian backgrounds.

In Seattle, such an opportunity has been developed by a Presbyterian pastor, J. Graley Taylor. After noting the many resources available for single adults in Seattle which provide therapy, support, and growth experiences, Taylor proposed that there was a missing element. He suggested, and obtained, presbytery and interdenominational support for "the development of an on-going community that meets emotional, social, and spiritual needs of those from moderate and liberal mainline churches."[35]

"The community has a celebrational style of worship as its core experience," and seeks to "express its witness in concerns for justice and reconciliation." It is open to all single adults: never-married, separated, divorced, widowed of all ages. It is ecumenical, open and receptive to churched and unchurched. "The Community" proposes that it is "a fellowship beyond the local parish that supports participation in the home parish and provides a supplemental, noncompetitive Christian community for singles."[36]

Worship celebrations generally are in homes, similar to "the house church" experience of many communities. Its style is a celebration of wholeness and reconciliation. There is "an open recognition that Christ discovers us in our brokenness, and leads us toward wholeness."[37]

SUMMARY

In most communities, the church has failed to develop a ministry with single adults which is supportive and sensitive to their needs. The impression that many singles have is that the church does not care about them, primarily because they are not married.

Churches and communities that are concerned about developing a ministry with single adults can best do so by working through a process of listening and decision-making. Out of this process can emerge appropriate forms of ministry.

Churches need to explore carefully their motives for entering into a stronger ministry with singles. Goals need to be developed that take into consideration the particular needs of the single adults they want to serve. Those needs may vary, depending upon the concentration of young singles, divorced and separated, widowed, and never-married. They will have to decide whether or not a ministry would most effectively be carried out by a single congregation or by ecumenical or inter-church effort. Cooperative or ecumenical ministries may be the most viable direction for smaller churches, which have a concern for singles but lack the resources. There also are many possibilities for a nongroup ministry with singles, starting with consciousness-raising efforts and adequate resourcing.

Alternatives to starting "singles groups" might be looked at and developed. Among the options are extended family opportunities, as well as some forms of Christian communal arrangements.

The church needs to look seriously at ways in which it can provide more inclusive worship/celebration opportunities for single adults. New expressions of worship related to divorce and remarriage may be developed, as well as ways found to support singles beyond the implications of Baptism.

7

THE CHALLENGE OF A NEW AGE

THE AGE in which we live may well be a major time of transition between an old style of living and a new.

It is a time when the institution of marriage is being tested from many directions, both outside and within. At the same time an increasing number of single adults are emerging in our culture. As in the past, many of them are looking to the church for direction and a sense of wholeness. Consequently, the church is caught with the double task of having to provide a sense of stability and direction for those who are married as well as to find appropriate ways to minister to those who are not.

The institution of marriage may well be changing in that process. The influence of the women's movement, the assertiveness of the homosexual community for legal, religious, and social acceptance, the increasing voice of single adults, and growing divorce rates are all forcing those who are married to look deeply into what the institution of marriage should be. Many traditional male-female roles are being altered. The pressures upon a married couple "to be all things to each other" may be relaxing a bit.

While supporting those who are married and caught in this transition time, the church is finding itself also having to alter its thinking about singleness. It has provided a strong emphasis on marriage and family in the past, and it is now being challenged to parallel that ministry with an affirmation of singleness.

To do that, the church needs to open up its theology, rethinking its Biblical-theological starting points regarding marriage, divorce, singleness, and the meaning of personhood. Trusting God's Spirit to lead in that reordering is never an easy process. Yet the church historically has had to do so, as the demands of a changing age have pressed upon it.

The thrust of this book has been to look at some of the pressures being put upon both the church and culture in dealing with singleness. Having explored traditional pairing pressures upon singles, as well as the needs of the various categories of singles, we can conclude that, by and large, the church has not been providing an adequate ministry to single adults. Church leaders and decision makers have not been accurate in their understanding of single adult needs. Consequently, whatever efforts have been made to relate to single adults often have fallen short of the mark.

New directions for ministry with single adults need to be found. A theological affirmation of singleness, using some new starting points, can help lead to more satisfying styles of ministry. As local churches and groups of churches work on developing appropriate forms of ministry, basic questions relating to motives and goals, the makeup and needs of singles, as well as appropriate models of ministry, need to be addressed. Possibly new alternatives to the traditional singles group may emerge.

Living "between the times" is never easy. It requires an act of faith and trust. There are no assurances that the ways we have traditionally done things will exist in the same form(s) in the new age. There are no guarantees that what has been "successful" in the past or present will work in the future. The church has to be free to risk, to try on new life-styles, to be a yeast in the leaven of human living. That analogy may be appropriate to the task facing the church as it seeks to provide a stronger base and shape for single adults in its worship and ministry.

The hope with which the church moves toward the future is the faithfulness and compassion of a loving God. God's concern is for whole persons, for community, for love and justice. God's creative Spirit calls, prods, and leads the people of God, whether married or single, along the journey of faith and life.

> Thus says the Lord . . .
> Behold, I am doing a new thing;
>   now it springs forth, do you not perceive it?
> I will make a way in the wilderness
>   and rivers in the desert.
> (Isa. 43:16, 19)

THE SINGLES MANIFESTO

PREAMBLE: Whereas the written and spoken word about singles has been and continues to be one of gloom and doom, untruths and misinformation, we the singles of the United States—divorced, separated, widowed and never-married—in order to bury the myths, establish the truths, uplift our spirits, promote our freedom, become cognizant of our great fortune as singles, do ordain and establish this manifesto for the singles of the United States of America.

ARTICLE I

Attitude toward self:

1. As a single, I shall appreciate myself as a unique person with a special combination of traits and talents no one else has.
2. I will develop and maintain a healthy self-respect and a high sense of self-worth, knowing that I cannot respect and like others until I first appreciate myself.
3. I will at all times take responsibility for my own actions, knowing that responsibility begins within my own self.
4. I will strive to put all my talents to work so that I can

Excerpted from *The Challenge of Being Single*, pp. 215–217, by Marie Edwards and Eleanor Hoover, © 1974 by Marie Edwards and Eleanor Hoover, published by New American Library. Used by permission of J. P. Tarcher, Inc.

eliminate any residual, socially induced feelings of inferiority, knowing that when I give of myself to others, my self-esteem will rise accordingly.

5. I will have goals, knowing I will feel a sense of elation and heightened self-esteem once the goal is accomplished.

6. I will give myself rewards when I have accomplished a goal or difficult task, knowing the more I practice the spirit of giving to myself, the more I will be able to give to others —and rewards, like charity, begin at home.

7. I will take an entirely new look at loneliness, knowing there is a vast difference between loneliness and being alone, realizing further that loneliness is a part of the human condition and that facing it when it happens will allow me to appreciate the positive side of being alone.

8. I will, in my deepest feelings, know that it's okay to be single and, becoming braver, know that it's even more than okay —it can be a great and untapped opportunity for continuous personal growth.

ARTICLE II

Attitude toward others:

1. I will stop searching for the "one-and-only," knowing that as I become more free to be myself, I will be freer to care about others, so that relationships will come to me as a natural consequence and I will feel free to accept or reject them.

2. Instead of searching for the "one-and-only," I will realize the tremendous importance of friendships and will develop understanding, worthwhile friends of both the same and opposite sex. I will realize that platonic friendships are not only possible, but a necessary part of a successful single life.

3. I will take inventory of my present "friends," bypassing those who are negative and harmful and cultivating

those who are helpful and nourishing.
4. I will, when I attend singles' affairs, consider the singles I meet there as potential friends, not as "losers," knowing my attitude will color my perception even before I step in the door.

ARTICLE III

Attitude toward society:
1. I will appreciate that all four categories of singlehood— divorced, separated, widowed, and never-married—suffer similar discriminations and that we are much more alike than different, no matter what our age or sex.
2. I will appreciate that the so-called battle of the sexes is a social myth, that men and women are much more alike than different in their reaction to fear, rejection, loneliness, sorrow, joy, caring, sharing, and loving, and that, as singles, we have a unique opportunity to foster understanding and empathy between male and female.
3. I will no longer suffer in silence the injustices to me as a single, but will do everything I can to help eradicate them.
4. I will, by choosing to live a free single life, be helping to raise the status of singlehood. In doing this, I will be strengthening rather than weakening marriage, for when we truly have the option not to marry, marriage will be seen as a free choice rather than one demanded by a pairing society.
5. Finally, I will do my part in every way to promote good will between marrieds and singles, because misunderstandings will be diminished only when each of us, as a unique human being, realizes that being self-aware, autonomous, free, self-fulfilled, and whole has nothing whatsoever to do with being either married or single, but, in the final analysis, comes from being ourselves.

NOTES

Preface

1. U.S. Bureau of the Census, *Current Population Reports,* Series P-20, No. 306, "Marital Status and Living Arrangements: March 1976" (Washington, D.C.: U.S. Government Printing Office, 1977), pp. 132–141.

Chapter 1. Let's Form a Singles Group

1. Marvin Mayers, quoted by William Lyon, *A Pew for One, Please,* p. 36.

2. Lyon, *A Pew for One, Please,* p. 24.

3. Britton Wood, "The Formerly Married: The Church's New Frontier," in Gary R. Collins (ed.), *It's O.K. to Be Single,* p. 73.

4. *Report of the Task Force on the Single Adult in the Church,* Raymond Kay Brown, chairperson (Church Council of Greater Seattle and Associated Ministries of Tacoma-Pierce County, April 1977), p. 1.

5. *Ibid.,* p. 1.

6. Mark W. Lee, "The Church and the Unmarried," in Collins (ed.), *It's O.K. to Be Single,* pp. 50–55.

7. Wood, in Collins (ed.), *It's O.K. to Be Single,* p. 81.

8. Anne T. Hagen, "Five Ways to Help Single Persons and Those Who Suffer the Pain of Divorce," *The Lutheran Standard,* Jan. 18, 1977, p. 6.

9. *Ibid.*

10. Howard J. Clinebell, Jr., *The Mental Health Ministry of the Local Church,* p. 205.

11. Lyon, *A Pew for One, Please,* p. 92.

12. *Ibid.,* p. 88.

13. *Ibid.,* p. 90.

14. *Ibid.,* p. 19.

15. *Ibid.,* p. 98.

16. *Minutes of the 189th General Assembly,* Part I, *Journal* (Office of the General Assembly, The United Presbyterian Church U.S.A., 1977), p. 96.

Chapter 2. SURELY YOU PLAN TO GET MARRIED!

1. Gail Parent, *Sheila Levine Is Dead and Living in New York* (Bantam Books, 1973), p. 3.

2. *Ibid.*

3. *Ibid.,* p. 141.

4. Marie Edwards and Eleanor Hoover, *The Challenge of Being Single* (New American Library, Signet Books, 1975), p. 34.

5. Terri Williams, "The Forgotten Alternative in I Cor. 7," *Christianity Today,* May 25, 1973.

6. Carole Klein, *The Single Parent Experience,* p. 267.

7. Edwards and Hoover, *The Challenge of Being Single,* p. 14.

8. Paul Glick, "A Demographer Looks at American Families," *Journal of Marriage and the Family,* February 1975, p. 24.

9. *Ibid.*

10. *Ibid.,* p. 17.

11. Donald R. Allen, *Barefoot in the Church* (John Knox Press, 1972), p. 47.

12. Emil Brunner, *The Divine Imperative,* tr. by Olive Wyon, p. 350.

13. Roy W. Fairchild and John Charles Wynn, *Families in the Church,* p. 76.

14. Pierre L'Huillier, "Clerical Celibacy," *Eastern Churches Re-*

view, quoted in *Religious and Theological Abstracts,* Vol. 15, No. 1 (Spring 1972).

15. Charles A. Frazee, "The Origin of Clerical Celibacy in the Western Church," *Church History,* Vol. 41 (1972), pp. 149–167.

16. Herbert J. Miles, *Sexual Understanding Before Marriage,* p. 177.

17. Hagen, "Five Ways to Help Single Persons," p. 6.

18. Clinebell, *The Mental Health Ministry of the Local Church,* p. 205.

19. *Ibid.*

Chapter 3. YOU MUST BE LONELY A LOT

1. Herbert Passin, quoted by Edwards and Hoover, *The Challenge of Being Single,* p. 34.

2. Edwards and Hoover, *The Challenge of Being Single,* p. 113.

3. *Ibid.,* p. 118.

4. *Ibid.,* pp. 215–217.

5. Dag Hammarskjöld, *Markings,* tr. by Leif Sjöberg and W. H. Auden, p. 85.

6. Letha Scanzoni and Nancy Hardesty, *All We're Meant to Be,* p. 163.

7. Clara Thompson, "The Unmarried Woman," *Pastoral Psychology,* April 1959, p. 42.

8. Wes Bryan, "The Journey Isn't Over," *Faith at Work,* October 1974, p. 12.

9. Scanzoni and Hardesty, *All We're Meant to Be,* p. 163.

10. Information obtained from file research and interview with Walt West, manager of Better Business Bureau, Tacoma, Washington, Feb. 17, 1977.

11. *BBB Bulletin FACTS,* June 1973, published by Better Business Bureau, Tacoma, Washington.

12. Krishnamurti, quoted by Edwards and Hoover, *The Challenge of Being Single,* p. 82.

13. Bruce Larson, "The Gift of Loneliness," *Faith at Work,* October 1974, p. 26.

14. Mel Krantzler, *Creative Divorce*, p. 150.

15. Edwards and Hoover, *The Challenge of Being Single*, p. 79.

16. Gail Sheehy, *Passages*, p. 350.

17. Nancy Hardesty, "Being Single in Today's World," in Collins (ed.), *It's O.K. to Be Single*, p. 17.

18. Krantzler, *Creative Divorce*, p. 112.

19. Jim Smoke, *Growing Through Divorce*, p. 75.

20. Edwards and Hoover, *The Challenge of Being Single*, p. 203.

21. *Ibid.*

22. *Ibid.*, p. 52.

23. *Ibid.*

24. Cited by Susan Jacoby, "49 Million Singles Can't Be All Right," *The New York Times Magazine*, Feb. 17, 1974, p. 48.

25. Edwards and Hoover, *The Challenge of Being Single*, p. 52.

26. *U.S. News & World Report*, Oct. 7, 1974, p. 54.

27. "Rising Problems of Single Parents," *U.S. News & World Report*, July 16, 1973, p. 34.

28. *Consumer Survival Kit*, "Going It Alone: A Look at the Single Life" (Maryland Center for Public Broadcasting, 1976), p. 17.

29. *Sexuality and the Human Community* (Office of the General Assembly, The United Presbyterian Church U.S.A., 1970), p. 36.

30. Jacoby, "49 Million Singles," p. 43.

31. *Sexuality and the Human Community*, p. 35.

32. Williams, "The Forgotten Alternative in I Cor. 7," p. 7.

33. *Ibid.*, p. 8.

34. *Sexuality and the Human Community*, p. 36.

35. *Ibid.*, p. 35.

36. Linda LeSourd, "Living Creatively: The Single Woman and the Church," in Collins (ed.), *It's O.K. to Be Single*, p. 30.

37. *Sexuality and the Human Community*, p. 10.

38. Edwards and Hoover, *The Challenge of Being Single*, p. 184.

39. *Sexuality and the Human Community*, p. 15.

40. *Ibid.*

41. Hardesty, in Collins (ed.), *It's O.K. to Be Single*, p. 18.

42. Krantzler, *Creative Divorce*, p. 215.

43. Lee, in Collins (ed.), *It's O.K. to Be Single*, pp. 54–55.

44. Ashley Montagu, quoted by Edwards and Hoover, *The Challenge of Being Single*, p. 20.

45. Klein, *The Single Parent Experience*, p. 30.

46. *Ibid.*, p. 32.

47. *Ibid.*

48. Krantzler, *Creative Divorce*, p. 213.

49. Lyon, *A Pew for One, Please*, p. 94.

50. Krantzler, *Creative Divorce*, p. 215.

51. Dan Peterman, Carl Ridley, and Scott Anderson, "A Comparison of Cohabiting and Noncohabiting College Students," *Journal of Marriage and the Family*, August 1974, p. 354.

52. Krantzler, *Creative Divorce*, p. 232.

53. Edwards and Hoover, *The Challenge of Being Single*, p. 187.

54. Judith Krantz, "Living Together Is a Rotten Idea," *Cosmopolitan*, October 1976, p. 218.

55. Karen Durbin, "Premarital Divorce," *Harper's Magazine*, May 1974, p. 8.

.*Chapter* 4. SINGLES ARE SWINGERS

1. Jacoby, "49 Million Singles," p. 13.

2. Edwards and Hoover, *The Challenge of Being Single*, p. 18.

3. Jacoby, "49 Million Singles," p. 41.

4. Sheehy, *Passages*, pp. 237 and 198.

5. *Ibid.*

6. *Ibid.*, p. 199.

7. Warren Farrell, *The Liberated Man* (Bantam Books, 1975), p. 66.

8. Sheehy, *Passages*, p. 238.

9. Edwards and Hoover, *The Challenge of Being Single*, p. 19.

10. *Ibid.*, pp. 66–67.

11. *Ibid.*, p. 67.

12. Glick, "A Demographer Looks at American Families," p. 22. Glick quotes a figure from the U.S. Center for Health Statistics.

13. Jacoby, "49 Million Singles," p. 41.

14. Edwards and Hoover, *The Challenge of Being Single*, p. 42.

15. Glick, "A Demographer Looks at American Families," p. 23.

16. Edwards and Hoover, *The Challenge of Being Single*, findings by Dr. Thomas Holmes, p. 77.

17. Smoke, *Growing Through Divorce*, p. 106.

18. Krantzler, *Creative Divorce*, p. 78.

19. *Ibid.*, p. 30.

20. *Ibid.*, p. 12.

21. Smoke, *Growing Through Divorce*, p. 96.

22. Krantzler, *Creative Divorce*, p. 31.

23. Smoke, *Growing Through Divorce*, p. 106.

24. Krantzler, *Creative Divorce*, p. 215.

25. *Ibid.*, p. 108.

26. *Ibid.*, p. 110.

27. Garner Scott Odell, "A Study of Divorce Among Church Members in San Francisco Presbytery, The United Presbyterian Church U.S.A., with Implications for Ministry" (D. Min. dissertation, San Francisco Theological Seminary, 1975), p. 77.

28. George Buttrick (ed.), *The Interpreter's Bible*, Vol. 7, p. 299.

29. Alexander Jones (ed.), *The Jerusalem Bible*, p. 47.

30. Odell, "A Study of Divorce Among Church Members," p. 84.

31. *Ibid.*, p. 110.

32. Wood, in Collins (ed.), *It's O.K. to Be Single*, p. 71.

33. Lynn Caine, *Widow*.

34. *Ibid.*, p. 80. (Italics added.)

35. Alan Richardson (ed.), *A Theological Word Book of the Bible*, p. 281.

36. Wood, in Collins (ed.), *It's O.K. to Be Single*, p. 72.

37. Betty Bryant, *Leaning Into the Wind*, p. 2.

38. Caine, *Widow*, p. 60.

39. Bryant, *Leaning Into the Wind*, p. 5.

40. Caine, *Widow*, p. 140.

41. *Ibid.*, p. 90.

42. Bryant, *Leaning Into the Wind*, p. 44.

43. Caine, *Widow*, p. 79.

44. Sheehy, *Passages*, p. 344.

45. Patricia O'Brien, *The Woman Alone*, p. 69.

46. Scott Hope, "And So On (A Beginning to Work On)," paper prepared for Consultation on Young Adult Ministries, sponsored jointly by The United Presbyterian Church U.S.A. and the Presbyterian Church U.S., held in Dallas, Texas, December 1975.

47. "Serving Singles—Don't Play Mix and Match," editorial, *Christianity Today*, June 4, 1976, p. 29.

48. *Ibid.*

49. Hope, "And So On," p. 1.

50. From the paper prepared by the Youth Relations Unit, Program Agency, The United Presbyterian Church U.S.A., March 27, 1974.

51. Sheehy, *Passages*, p. 58.

52. *Ibid.*, p. 57.

53. David L. Erb, "Faith Development and the Implications for the Church," mimeographed address, May 1975.

54. *Ibid.*

55. Sheehy, *Passages*, p. 59.

56. Erb, "Faith Development," p. 6.

57. *Ibid.*, p. 3.

58. Hope, "And So On," p. 3.

59. *U.S. News & World Report*, Oct. 7, 1974.

60. Hope, "And So On," p. 8.

61. Sheehy, *Passages*, p. 63.

62. Lauri Warder, "How to Reach Me," *The Christian Ministry*, March 1976, p. 7.

63. *Ibid.*

64. "Rising Problems of 'Single Parents,' " *U.S. News & World Report*, July 16, 1973, p. 32. Figures cited are from U.S. Census Bureau, 1970.

65. "Single Mothers Struggle Against the Odds," *Tacoma News-Tribune*, May 4, 1976, p. A-18.

66. *Ibid.*

67. Scanzoni and Hardesty, *All We're Meant to Be*, p. 162.

68. Susan Griffin, "Confessions of a Single Mother," *Ramparts*, April 1973, p. 43.

69. Wood, in Collins (ed.), *It's O.K. to Be Single*, p. 74.

70. Edwards and Hoover, *The Challenge of Being Single,* p. 75.

71. Robert Pinder, "The Single-Parent Family and the Church," in Collins (ed.), *It's O.K. to Be Single,* p. 93.

72. *Ibid.,* p. 94.

73. Klein, *The Single Parent Experience,* p. 133.

74. Krantzler, *Creative Divorce,* p. 176.

75. Kenneth Barringer, "Focus: The Single Parent," *The Christian Home,* November 1972, p. 37, summarizing a seminar address by James Ewing.

76. Pinder, in Collins (ed.), *It's O.K. to Be Single,* p. 75.

77. Wood, in Collins (ed.), *It's O.K. to Be Single,* p. 74.

Chapter 5. As a Single, Could I Find Help from the Bible?

1. *Report of the Task Force on the Single Adult in the Church,* p. 5.

2. Hardesty, in Collins (ed.), *It's O.K. to Be Single,* p. 13.

3. *The Interpreter's Dictionary of the Bible,* Supplementary Volume (Abingdon Press, 1976), p. 573.

4. *The Interpreter's Bible,* Vol. 7, p. 482.

5. Lee, in Collins (ed.), *It's O.K. to Be Single,* p. 49.

6. Matthew Black and H. H. Rowley (eds.), *Peake's Commentary on the Bible,* p. 957. See also commentary in *IDB,* Sup. Vol., p. 576, and W. Robertson Nicoll (ed.), *The Expositor's Bible,* Vol. 4, p. 664.

7. *IDB,* Sup. Vol., p. 577.

8. Philip Schaff, *History of the Christian Church,* Vol. 1, p. 44.

9. Hardesty, in Collins (ed.), *It's O.K. to Be Single,* p. 15.

10. *Ibid.,* p. 7.

11. Rosemary R. Ruether, "Women's Liberation in Historical and Theological Perspective," in Sarah B. Doely (ed.), *Women's Liberation and the Church,* p. 36.

12. Darrell J. Doughty, "Homosexuality and Obedience to the Gospel," *Church and Society,* The United Presbyterian Church U.S.A., May-June 1977, p. 13.

13. *Ibid.,* p. 15.

14. *Ibid.,* p. 18.

15. John H. Yoder, "Singleness in Ethical and Pastoral Perspective," (Mennonite Biblical Seminary, 1973), p. 1.

16. Lee, in Collins (ed.), *It's O.K. to Be Single,* p. 49.

17. Paul Hinnebusch, quoted by Hardesty, in Collins (ed.), *It's O.K. to Be Single,* p. 12.

18. Gerhard Friedrich (ed.), *Theological Dictionary of the New Testament,* Vol. 2, p. 156.

19. *Ibid.,* p. 164.

20. Hardesty, in Collins (ed.), *It's O.K. to Be Single,* p. 12.

21. Dietrich Bonhoeffer, *Life Together,* p. 25.

22. *The Book of Order,* The United Presbyterian Church U.S.A. (Office of the General Assembly, 1967), 20.01. See also Rom. 6:3 and Col. 2:12.

23. *Ibid.,* 21.02.

24. Dietrich Bonhoeffer, *The Cost of Discipleship,* p. 113.

25. LeSourd, in Collins (ed.), *It's O.K. to Be Single,* p. 26.

26. *Ibid.*

27. Bonhoeffer, *Life Together,* p. 30.

28. *Ibid.,* p. 38.

29. Confession of 1967, *The Book of Confessions,* 9.22.

30. LeSourd in Collins (ed.), *It's O.K. to Be Single,* p. 25.

31. Frieda Armstrong, *To Be Free,* p. 120.

Chapter 6. WHAT FORM SHALL A SINGLES MINISTRY TAKE?

1. Lyon, *A Pew for One, Please,* p. 42.

2. *Ibid.,* p. 43.

3. *Ibid.,* p. 42.

4. *Solo Center News,* published by the Solo Center, Seattle, Washington, October 1976.

5. *Ibid.,* p. 67.

6. *Ibid.,* p. 68.

7. *Ibid.,* p. 71.

8. *Ibid.,* p. 80.

9. *Ibid.,* p. 84.

10. *Ibid.,* p. 95.

11. Wood, in Collins (ed.), *It's O.K. to Be Single*, p. 70.

12. Virginia McIver, "Learning to Live Alone: The Divorced Person and the Church," in Collins (ed.), *It's O.K. to Be Single*, pp. 61–62.

13. Lyon, *A Pew for One, Please*, p. 89.

14. Wood, in Collins (ed.), *It's O.K. to Be Single*, p. 77.

15. *Ibid.*, p. 78.

16. Hagen, "Five Ways to Help Single Persons," p. 7.

17. Odell, "A Study of Divorce Among Church Members," p. 96.

18. Bylaws of Tacoma Area Singles Center, sponsored by the Associated Ministries of Tacoma-Pierce County, adopted April 12, 1977, Article III.

19. Otis E. Young, "A Church Ministering to Singles," *The Christian Ministry*, March 1976, p. 9.

20. *Ibid.*

21. Britton Wood, "The Formerly Married: The Church's New Frontier," *Theology, News, and Notes*, Fuller Theological Seminary, March 1976, p. 18.

22. *Report of the Task Force on the Single Adult in the Church.*

23. Yoder, "Singleness in Ethical and Pastoral Perspective," p. 5.

24. Caine, *Widow*, p. 82.

25. Klein, *The Single Parent Experience*, p. 237.

26. James E. Symons' response on a questionnaire sent to the Community for Christian Celebration, Olympia, Washington, during my dissertation project research.

27. Description provided by extended family participant, Pat Stere, coleader at Ghost Ranch Singles Seminar, August 1976.

28. Allen, *Barefoot in the Church*, p. 48.

29. William M. Kephart, *Extraordinary Groups*, p. 283.

30. Yoder, "Singleness in Ethical and Pastoral Perspective," p. 4.

31. *Ibid.*

32. Maggie Kuhn, lecture at Whitworth College, Spokane, Washington, Feb. 16, 1978.

33. Allen, *Barefoot in the Church*, p. 128.

34. See Hoyt Hickman, *Ritual in a New Day,* p. 73f.

35. J. Graley Taylor, "Proposal for an Experimental Ministry to Single Adults" (Seattle, Washington, 1977), p. 2.

36. *Ibid.*

37. Interview with J. Graley Taylor.

BIBLIOGRAPHY

American Bible Society. *Good News Bible: The Bible in Today's English Version.* 1976.

Armstrong, Frieda. *To Be Free.* Fortress Press, 1974.

Associated Ministries of Tacoma-Pierce County. Bylaws of Tacoma Area Singles Center. Adopted April 12, 1977.

Barringer, Kenneth. "Focus: The Single Parent," *The Christian Home,* November 1972.

Bernard, Jessie. *The Future of Marriage.* Bantam Books, 1973.

Black, Matthew, and Rowley, H. H., eds. *Peake's Commentary on the Bible.* London: Thomas Nelson & Sons, 1962.

Bonhoeffer, Dietrich. *The Cost of Discipleship.* Translated by R. H. Fuller. Macmillan Co., 1959.

————. *Life Together.* Translated and with an introduction by John W. Doberstein. Harper & Brothers, 1954.

Bosmajian, Hamida, and Bosmajian, Haig A., eds. *This Great Argument: The Rights of Women.* Addison-Wesley Publishing Co., 1972.

Breen, Paula. "Singles Face the Issues," *Faith at Work,* October 1974.

Brunner, Emil. *The Divine Imperative.* Westminster Press, 1947.

Bryant, Betty. *Leaning Into the Wind.* Fortress Press, 1975.

Buttrick, George, ed. *The Interpreter's Bible.* 12 vols. Abingdon-Cokesbury Press, 1952.

―――. *The Interpreter's Dictionary of the Bible.* 4 vols. Abingdon Press, 1962.

Caine, Lynn. *Widow.* William Morrow & Co., 1974.

The Christian Science Monitor, "Being Single in the U.S.," Dec. 10, 1974.

Christianity Today, editorial, "Celebrate Singleness—Marriage May Be Second Best," May 7, 1976.

Christianity Today, editorial, "Serving Singles—Don't Play Mix and Match," June 4, 1976.

Christoff, Nicholas. *Saturday Night, Sunday Morning: Singles and the Church.* Harper & Row, 1978.

Church Council of Greater Seattle, *Report of the Task Force on the Single Adult in the Church.* Raymond Kay Brown, chairperson. April 1977.

Clinebell, Howard J., Jr. *The Mental Health Ministry of the Local Church.* Abingdon Press, 1962.

―――. *The People Dynamic.* Harper & Row, 1972.

Collins, Gary R., ed. *It's O.K. to Be Single: A Guidebook for Singles and the Church.* Word Books, 1976.

Decker, Bea. "They Help Each Other." *Faith at Work,* October 1976.

Doely, Sarah Bentley, ed. *Women's Liberation and the Church.* Association Press, 1970.

Dunne, John S. *Time and Myth.* Doubleday & Co., 1973.

Durbin, Karen. "Premarital Divorce," *Harper's Magazine,* May 1974.

Edwards, Marie. Town Hall Series, Tacoma, Washington. Interview and lecture, March 1976.

―――. "What It Takes to Succeed on One's Own," *The Christian Science Monitor,* Dec. 13, 1974.

―――, and Hoover, Eleanor. *The Challenge of Being Single.* J. P. Tarcher, Inc., 1974; New American Library, Signet Books, 1975.

Erb, David L. "Faith Development and the Implications for the Church." Address given at meeting of the Synod of Alaska-Northwest, Whitworth College, Spokane, May 1975. Mimeographed.

Fairchild, Roy W. *Christians in Families.* CLC Press, 1964.

————, and Wynn, John Charles. *Families in the Church: A Protestant Survey.* Association Press, 1961.

Farrell, Warren. *The Liberated Man.* Random House, 1975; Bantam Books, 1975.

Francoeur, Robert T. *Eve's New Rib.* Dell Publishing Co., 1972.

Friedrich, Gerhard, ed. *Theological Dictionary of the New Testament,* Vol. 9. Translated and edited by Geoffrey W. Bromiley. Wm. B. Eerdmans Publishing Co., 1974.

Frost, Heidi. "Who's the Lucky One?" *Faith at Work,* October 1974.

Gardner, Richard A. *The Boys and Girls Book About Divorce.* Science House, 1970; Bantam Books, 1971.

Glasser, William. *The Identity Society.* Harper & Row, Publishers, 1972.

Glazer, Nona, and Waehrer, Helen Youngelson, eds. *Woman in a Man-Made World.* 2d ed. Rand McNally & Co., 1977.

Glick, Paul. "A Demographer Looks at American Families," *Journal of Marriage and the Family,* February 1975.

Griffin, Susan. "Confessions of a Single Mother," *Ramparts,* April, 1973.

Hagen, Anne T. "Five Ways to Help Single Persons and Those Who Suffer the Pain of Divorce," *The Lutheran Standard,* Jan. 18, 1977.

Hammarskjöld, Dag. *Markings.* Translated by Leif Sjöberg and W. H. Auden. Foreword by W. H. Auden. Alfred A. Knopf, 1964.

Hardesty, Nancy A. "Marital Status: Single," *Daughters of Sarah,* January 1976.

Harris, Janet. *The Prime of Ms. America.* G. P. Putnam's Sons, 1975; New American Library, Signet Books, 1976.

Hastings, James, ed. *Dictionary of the Bible.* Rev. ed. by Frederick C. Grant and H. H. Rowley. Charles Scribner's Sons, 1963.

Hickman, Hoyt. *Ritual in a New Day.* Abingdon Press, 1976.

Holloway, Mark. *Heavens on Earth: Utopian Communities in America, 1680–1880.* Dover Publications, 1966.

Hope, Scott. "And So On (A Beginning to Work On.)" Paper. Consultation on Youg Adult Ministries, Dallas, Texas, December 1975.

The United Presbyterian Church U.S.A. and the Presbyterian Church U.S.

Huber, Milton. "Counseling the Single Woman," *Pastoral Psychology,* April 1959.

Hulme, Wm. E.; Polatin, Phillip; Hopper, Myron T.; and Rutledge, Aaron L. "Sexual Containment for the Unmarried," *Pastoral Psychology,* April 1959.

Jacoby, Susan. "49 Million Singles Can't Be All Right," *The New York Times Magazine,* Feb. 17, 1974.

Jewett, Paul K. *Man as Male and Female.* Wm. B. Eerdmans Publishing Co., 1975.

Jones, Alexander, ed. *The Jerusalem Bible.* Doubleday & Co., 1966.

Kanter, Rosabeth Moss. *Commitment and Community.* Harvard University Press, 1972.

Kephart, William M. *Extraordinary Groups.* St. Martin's Press, 1976.

Klein, Carole. *The Single Parent Experience.* Avon Books, 1973.

Krantz, Judith. "Living Together Is a Rotten Idea," *Cosmopolitan,* October 1976.

Krantzler, Mel. *Creative Divorce.* M. Evans & Co., 1973; New American Library, 1975.

Kuhn, Maggie. Lecture and interview, Whitworth College, Spokane, Washington, Feb. 16, 1978.

LaShan, Eda. *The Wonderful Crisis of Middle Age.* David McKay Co., 1973.

Levine, JoAnn. "One Out of Three U.S. Adults Are Single," *Tacoma News-Tribune,* Jan. 12, 1975.

Lyon, Bayard W. "Parents Without Partners," *The Christian Ministry,* March 1976.

Lyon, William. *A Pew for One, Please.* Seabury Press, 1977.

Maryland Center for Public Broadcasting. *Consumer Survival Kit,* "Going It Alone: A Look at the Single Life."

Miles, Herbert J. *Sexual Understanding Before Marriage.* Zondervan Publishing House, 1971.

Moustakas, Clark E. *Loneliness and Love.* Prentice-Hall, 1972.

National Council of Churches. *A Synoptic of Recent Denomina-*

tional Statements on Sexuality. 2d ed. Compiled by Wm. H. Genne, 1975. Mimeographed.

Newsweek, "Games Singles Play," July 16, 1973.

Nicoll, W. Robertson, ed. *The Expositor's Bible,* Vols. 4–5. Wilbur Ketchum Publisher, n.d.

Nouwen, Henri J. M. *The Wounded Healer.* Doubleday & Co., 1972.

O'Brien, Patricia. *The Woman Alone.* Quadrangle/New York Times Book Company, 1973.

Odell, Garner Scott, "A Study of Divorce Among Church Members in San Francisco Presbytery, The United Presbyterian Church U.S.A., with Implications for Ministry." D. Min. dissertation, San Francisco Theological Seminary, 1975.

Parent, Gail. *Sheila Levine Is Dead and Living in New York.* G. P. Putnam's Sons, 1972; Bantam Books, 1973.

Payne, Dorothy. *Women Without Men.* United Church Press, 1969.

Peterman, Dan; Ridley, Carl; and Anderson, Scott. "A Comparison of Cohabiting and Noncohabiting College Students," *Journal of Marriage and the Family,* August 1974.

Pruden, Wesley, Jr., "Singles Mistreated?" *The National Observer,* Feb. 28, 1976.

Ramey, James. *Intimate Friendships.* Prentice-Hall, 1976.

Richardson, Alan, ed. *A Theological Word Book of the Bible.* Macmillan Co., 1956.

Rosenblum, Arlene. "Weekend Mother," *The Single Parent,* April 1977, p. 14.

Scanzoni, Letha, and Hardesty, Nancy. *All We're Meant to Be.* Word Books, 1974.

Schaff, Philip. *History of the Christian Church.* Vol. 1. Wm. B. Eerdmans Publishing Co., 1910.

Seattle Times, "New Policies Urged to Respond to Changing Character of Seattle," Jan. 19, 1977.

Sheehy, Gail. "Catch 30 and Other Predictable Crises of Growing Up Adult," *New York Magazine,* Feb. 18, 1974.

———. *Passages.* E. P. Dutton & Co., 1974.

Simmons, Morgan. "Our Ministry to Singles," *The Christian Ministry,* March 1976.

Sinks, Robert F. "Theology of Divorce," *The Christian Century,* April 20, 1977.

Small, Dwight. *The Right to Remarry.* Fleming H. Revell, Co., 1975.

Smoke, Jim. *Growing Through Divorce.* Harvest House Publishers, 1976.

Solo Center News. Solo Center, Seattle, Washington, October 1976.

Spreitzer, Elmer, and Riley, Lawrence E. "Factors Associated with Singlehood," *Journal of Marriage and the Family,* August 1974.

Stephen, Beverly. "An Underground 'Marriage' in Court," *San Francisco Chronicle,* April 10, 1974.

Stringfellow, William. *Instead of Death.* Seabury Press, 1963.

Tacoma News-Tribune, "All the Lonely People," July 26–28, 1976.

Tacoma News-Tribune, "Single Mothers Struggle Against the Odds," May 4, 1976.

Taylor, J. Graley. "Proposal for an Experimental Ministry to Single Adults." Presbytery of Seattle, 1977.

Theology, News, and Notes, "Singles and the Church," March 1976. Published by Fuller Theological Seminary Alumni, Mary Tregenza, ed.

Thompson, Clara. "The Unmarried Woman," *Pastoral Psychology,* April 1959.

Tompkins, Iverna. *How to Make It in No Man's Land.* Logos International, 1975.

Tournier, Paul. *Escape from Loneliness.* Westminster Press, 1962.

United Church of Canada. *Marriage Breakdown, Divorce, Remarriage, A Christian Understanding.* Ontario: Board of Christian Education, 1962.

The United Presbyterian Church U.S.A. *The Constitution,* Part I: *The Book of Confessions.* Office of the General Assembly, 1966.

———. *The Constitution,* Part II: *The Book of Order.* Office of the General Assembly, 1967.

———. *Minutes of the 189th General Assembly,* Part I, *Journal.* Office of the General Assembly, 1977.

———. "Problem Pregnancies: Toward a Responsible Decision." Office of the General Assembly, 1977.

———. *Sexuality and the Human Community.* Office of the General Assembly, 1970.

———. "Some Guidelines for Ministry with Young Adults." Board of National Missions, 1970.

U.S. Bureau of the Census. *Current Population Reports,* Series P-20, No. 306, "Marital Status and Living Arrangements: March 1976." Washington, D.C.: U.S. Government Printing Office, 1977.

U.S. Department of the Treasury, Internal Revenue Service. *1977 Instructions for Form 1040.*

U.S. News & World Report, "Rise of the 'Singles'—40 Million Free Spenders," Oct. 7, 1974.

Warder, Lauri. "How to Reach Me," *The Christian Ministry,* March 1976.

Wiley, Martha. Tacoma, Washington. Interview, Feb. 6, 1977.

Williams, Terri. "The Forgotten Alternative in I Cor. 7," *Christianity Today,* May 25, 1973.

Yoder, John H. "Singleness in Ethical and Pastoral Perspective." Paper. Mennonite Biblical Seminary, 1973.

Young, Otis E. "A Church Ministering to Singles," *The Christian Ministry,* March 1976.

Young, Robert. *Analytical Concordance to the Bible.* Funk & Wagnalls Co., 1910.